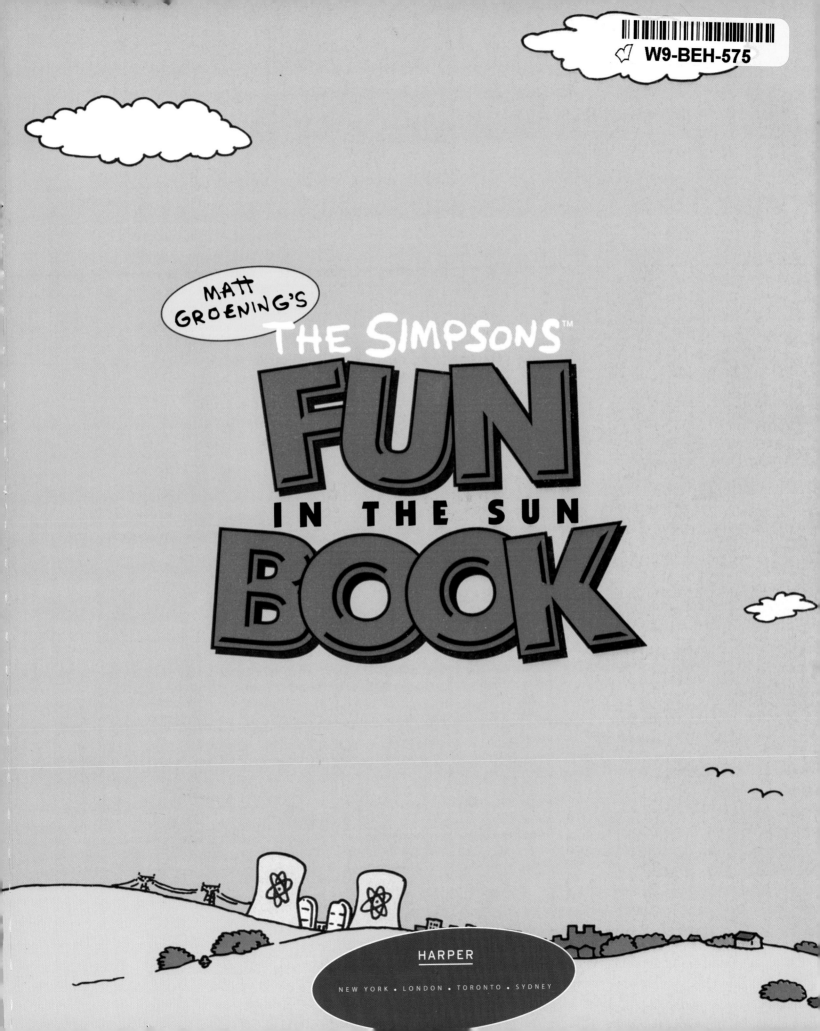

MATT GROENING'S

THE SIMPSONS™

FUN
IN THE SUN
BOOK

HARPER

NEW YORK · LONDON · TORONTO · SYDNEY

Dedicated to the memory of Snowball I:

Your kitty door has rusted,
but our love for you has not.

THE SIMPSONS RAINY DAY FUN BOOK was originally published in 1991 by HarperPerennial, a Division of HarperCollins Publishers. Copyright© 1991 by Matt Groening Productions, inc.

THE SIMPSONS FUN IN THE SUN BOOK was originally published in 1992 by HarperPerennial, a Division of HarperCollins Publishers. Copyright© 1992 by Matt Groening Productions, inc.

THE SIMPSONS ULTRA-JUMBO RAIN-OR-SHINE FUN BOOK. Copyright © 1993 by Matt Groening Productions, inc. All rights reserved. Printed in the United States of America. No part of this book may be used or reproduced in any manner whatsoever without written permission except in the case of brief quotations embodied in critical articles and reviews. For information address HarperCollins Publishers, 10 East 53rd Street, New York, NY 10022.

HarperCollins books may be purchased for educational, business, or sales promotional use. For information please write: Special Markets Department, HarperCollins Publishers, 10 East 53rd Street, New York, NY 10022.

First Harper paperback published 2006.

ISBN-10: 0-06-095006-4
ISBN-13: 978-0-06-095006-4

06 07 08 09 10 RRD 10 9 8 7 6 5 4 3 2

Concepts, Design & Art Direction: Cindy Vance
Design: Peter Alexander
Fun in the Sun Team: Mary Trainor, Peter Alexander, Steve Vance
Additional Research: Jamie Angell, Jan Strnad, Julie Strnad
Creative Team: Bill Morrison, Michael Polcino, Barbara McAdams, Adriana Galvez, Jen Kamerman
Legal Advisor: Susan Grode

If your mother is anything like ours, you're probably at the mercy of a lot of her mood swings. These usually result in your being ejected from the house on any number of trumped-up charges and thereby being forced to find some means of entertainment *other* than television.

Well, it was these sorts of everyday childhood disasters we had in mind when we put together this book. It was the thought of YOU, sitting blank-eyed and open-mouthed out on the back porch, that inspired us!

Mope no more, good people. For we have compiled a lifetime's worth of thrilling, pulse-racing, outdoor activities! We've got classic run-amok-all-over-the-neighborhood-type games like tag, hide 'n' seek, treasure hunts, scavenger hunts, and our own captivating "Slaves of the Space Mutants."

We've got artsy-craftsy stuff, too: knarly knot tying, face painting, potato printing, Ned Flanders' guide to building a better bird house, and cool kites and mobiles you can make yourself.

We've got the cold facts and hot tips on camping, road trips, and going to the beach or pool. We've even got a backyard carnival with a spook house, a bearded lady, and who knows what else! And lotsa mind-boggling, hair-raising, knee-jerking stuff you won't find anywhere else, like Bart's Brainless Bike-O-Rama, Otto's Weird Tale, Captain Lance Murdock's Daredevil Obstacle Course, and the spine-tingling, boot-licking Party at the Burns Mansion!

So, whether you're looking for an exciting way to spend your time, a leisurely way to pass your time, or just an idiotic way to waste your time, this, my friend, is the book for you!

THE THRILL OF THE CHASE

RUN-AROUND-TILL-YOU'RE-HOT-N-STICKY GAMES

If you are lucky enough to have a bunch of kids in your neighborhood, here are some games to play if you can get everybody together. Now you'll just have to agree on which game to play, man!

HIDE-N-SEEK

The mother of all outdoor group games. If you don't know how to play this game, you must have been born on Mars. But you're a clever enough Martian to have bought this book, so we'll explain it to you now and save you further embarrassment (or detection!). Choose someone to be "It" (an appropriate name for you aliens). Pick a tree, the front steps, or a lightpost for home base. "It" counts to 100 loudly while everyone else hides, then yells, "Ready or not, here I come! Anyone around this base is automatically 'It'." "It" then goes looking for all the hiders. If "It" sees someone, "It" runs to tag home, yelling "1, 2, 3, on (kid's name) in the (name of the place they're hiding)." If the person spotted can tag home before "It" gets there, that person is safe. But if "It" gets to home first, then the person spotted is "It" in the next game. The play continues until all players are found. The last one "It" tags is "It" in the next game. If "It" gives up and cannot find any more hiders, "It" yells, "All outs in free," the players come out of hiding, and "It" is "It" again for the next game. If you have any questions, ask anyone you know to explain it to you. They'll tell you how to play – – and ask if you were born on Mars!

25-30% OF AMERICAN CHILDREN ARE OVERWEIGHT, AN INCREASE OF 40% IN THE PAST TWENTY YEARS, OR SO SAYS A BUNCH OF CHUBBY STATISTICIANS.

Blindman's Bluff

Think of a creative way to chose someone to be "It." Now, blindfold and spin them around five times. The other players prance around "It," taunting and jeering and trying to come as close as possible without being touched. If "It" touches someone, that person immediately becomes "It" and you play again.

INSECTS DON'T HAVE NOSES.

WHEN A CAT DIED IN A HOUSE IN ANCIENT EGYPT, EVERYONE IN THE HOUSE SHAVED THEIR EYEBROWS.

Basic Tag

If you haven't played this, you might be from Saturn, not Mars! Mark off boundaries on a large, open area. Pick one person to be "It." Everybody else runs around, trying not to be tagged by "It" but staying within the bounds. Whoever gets tagged now becomes "It." The game continues until everyone gives up and goes inside to watch TV.

FREEZE TAG

Same as Basic Tag except that when "It" touches someone, they must "freeze" in that position. Any player not frozen can unfreeze frozen players by touching them. The game is over when everyone is frozen. The person frozen the longest is "It" in the next game.

Animal Tag

This is a particularly strange and funny version of Freeze Tag. When a player is tagged, "It" assigns them an animal to be. For example, she'll say, "You're a sheep," or a laughing hyena, a snake, or a mugwump. They must stand where they are and act like that animal until they are tagged by another player or the game is over. The game is over when everyone has been tagged. Be creative! This is a great way of making people look really stupid!

FLASHLIGHT TAG

This Film Noir cross between Tag and Hide-N-Seek is played at night. Pick an area with trees and bushes or other good obstacles to hide behind and dodge around. All players must have a flashlight. Everyone scatters around the playing area and tries to "tag" other players by shining a flashlight on them. If you're tagged, you're out. The last person left is the winner.

EACH HUMAN FOOT HAS ABOUT 7,200 SEPARATE NERVES.

THE CUSTOM OF SHAKING HANDS ORIGINATED IN THE PRACTICE OF ADVERSARIES GRASPING THE WEAPON HAND DURING A TRUCE AS A PRECAUTION AGAINST TREACHERY.

Shadow Tag

In the true spirit of this book, this game must be played on a sunny day. The player chosen as "It" chases the others and tries to tag one of them by stepping on their shadow! That player is then "It" and the game continues.

URBAN MANEUVERS

THE MYSTERY OF THE MARBLES

This is truly one of the oldest games around. Like, really old. Older than Mick Jagger, even. Your dad may not know how to play this one. In fact, we don't really even know how to play this one. But trust us, it's supposed to be loads of fun! The only problem is trying to find someone old enough who can still remember past what he had for breakfast and who can remember the rules to the darn thing. So here's the challenge. Buy some marbles, and search out the oldest man in your neighborhood (marbles was primarily a boys' game, back in the old days when things were divided like that). Show him your marbles, and ask him if he remembers how to play. Tell him you need to know or you'll join a gang. You might have to sit through some longwinded, senseless babbling about how things were so much better when he was a kid, but you just might learn something and have fun in the process. Besides, maybe his wife will give you some ribbon candy, just for being so patient with him.

SCAT CAT, SAVE THE RAT

This is a favorite of the younger set. As soon as Maggie can stand up for more than a minute and a half, she'll be out playing this game. Everyone stands facing each other forming a circle holding hands. One person is outside the circle — the cat — and one person is inside the circle — the rat. The cat tries to tag the rat but everyone tries to keep the cat outside the circle. The rat is the good guy in this game. Everyone helps the rat by lifting their arms to let it in and out of the circle, keeping it away from the cat. If the rat gets tagged, it becomes the cat, someone else becomes the rat, and you all play again. If the cat cannot tag the rat in one minute, another pair are chosen and the play continues again.

JUMPIN' JEHOVA-JACKS

You can either play with a store-bought set of jacks or use six small, smooth stones and a small rubber ball. There are many stages in the game, so decide before you start how many you want to go through. In each one, you begin by tossing the jacks out on the ground in front of you. The object is to throw the ball in the air, pick up the number of jacks indicated (and perform additional feats as required), and catch the ball again, after it has bounced once (and only once). And you must do all this using only one hand and without disturbing any other jacks! If you fail, you lose your turn but start again at that same stage on your next turn. The first player to finish all the stages successfully wins. The basic stages begin with "Onesies." You throw the ball up, pick up one jack, and catch the ball. Put the jack aside and continue until you've picked them all up, one at a time. Then go to "Twosies" – same action, but you're picking up two at a time. You can pluck them separately as long as you use one hand and still catch the ball before it bounces twice. Then go to "Threesies," "Foursies," "Fivesies," and finally "Sixies," where you grab all of them at once. Now repeat the stages with twists added. In "Pats," you throw the ball up, pat the ground, and pick up the jacks. For "Double Pats," pat the ground twice. In "Pigs in the Pen," form a "pen" with your non-throwing hand as shown. Instead of picking up the jacks, you slide them over into the pen. In "Over the Fence," place the jacks on the far side of the hand forming the pen. In "Birds in the Nest," hold your non-throwing hand palm up and place the jacks in the "nest" formed as you collect them. Make up your own challenging variations!

Fig. 1

ONE OUT OF EVERY
HUNDRED AMERICANS
IS NAMED SMITH.

NO-FAULT FOUR SQUARE

Draw four connecting squares on the ground, making each one at least three feet on each side. Mark them A, B, C, and D. A player stands in each one. Player D starts the game by bouncing a large rubber ball or a basketball over to player A. The ball must bounce once in the receiver's square before he in turn hits it into another player's square. If any player misses the ball, or hits it outside a square or on a line, the play stops and that player moves down a square (from D to C, for example; A is the "lowest" square). Any player "below" him moves up. If player A makes a mistake, she must exit the game, go to the end of the line, and let another player in to take her place.

The object is to stay in the game the longest. A simpler version of this game for the littlest of players is called "Two Square." It is played the same way, but with two squares instead of four. This is great for developing coordination skills in your younger brothers or sisters. When they get better, you can beat them in Four Square!

OFF THE WALL BALL

Find a big, blank wall space with no windows in it! Draw a big square on the ground coming out from the wall, about fifteen feet on each side. Two people play this game. It's like handball or raquetball; each player hits the ball with his hand against the wall, and the other player must return it it in the same fashion, without going outside the square. The ball can also only bounce once before you hit it. You use a big rubber ball, or you could substitute a basketball, and play that you catch and throw the ball, instead of hitting it in a continuous play.

HOPSCOTCH

The classic sidewalk game of all time. This game was supposedly invented by Napoleon while crossing the Alps, but the French take credit for everything so We may never really know. Draw a grid on the sidewalk as shown in the illustration. Throw a token of some sort into the first square and hop on one foot over it into each other square till you reach the top of the grid. Now turn and go back to the start the same way. You cannot hop into any square that has yours or someone else's token in it. The only time your other foot can touch the ground is when you get to the two squares side by side. When you get back to square one (a popular expression this game inspired), pick up your token and hop into square one (as long as no one else's token is in it) before hopping out. If you complete this successfully, throw your token into square two and go again. If you or your token touch a line at any time during your play, you forfeit your turn and it's the next player's turn. The first player to advance their token all the way to the last square wins.

PAVEMENT PICASSO

Another pastime inspired by the French, although Dick Van Dyke's character did quite a fine job of it in "Mary Poppins" and he was British. But anyone can do it, actually. All you need is some pavement and some colored chalks. Let your imagination flow! Draw landscapes, portraits of your friends or your teacher, or your favorite TV characters! The only thing that can stop you is a sudden rainstorm.

GUTTER BOATS
Running out of things to float down the gutter? Turn pro. Try these boats!

WALNUT BOATS
Take half of a nut and float it with the open side up. Add a sail of paper and a small twig for a mast.

POPSICLE STICK RAFT
Use two sticks as cross braces. Glue more sticks across them as shown. If you don't have popsicle sticks, regular sticks will do just fine.

Decorate Your Bike!!

No, you don't need glasses – these instructions refer to the stuff on the other side of this page. Cut out the Itchy and Scratchy cards and attach them to the fork or fender of your bike (try clothespins or tape) so the spokes of the wheels batter them as they go 'round and 'round – Itchy and Scratchy like that! Then cut out the Bart head and tape it around the front part of your bike like a headlight. Ride on!

CREATE YOUR OWN OFFICIAL
CAPTAIN LANCE MURDOCK DEATH-DEFYING
Daredevil OBSTACLE COURSE!

Hey, skateboarders! I may not know an ollie from a stan, but I do know pain when I meet it face to face. That's why I'm telling you the key to running any obstacle course is to AVOID THE OBSTACLES! Now, once you've set up your course, like the one Bart has here, try timing yourself and your friends to see who can go around the course the fastest. And remember, if you can't go over 'em, go around 'em — but *never* attempt to go through 'em! And I'm talkin' from experience here, kids!

GO AHEAD AND JUMP! SEE IF I CARE

(I CAN SEE YOUR UNDERWEAR!)

Rhyming songs help you keep your rhythm going as you're jumping rope.
Here are a few to get you started. Make up your own.

Three, six, nine
Goose drank wine,
Monkey chewed tobacco
On the street car line.
The line broke,
The monkey got choked
And they all went to heaven
In a little row boat!
Clap! Clap!

———

Drat that cat that
Trapped that rat.

Bag that hag that
Ragged that flag.

Splat that brat that
Zapped that hat.

Stop that cop that
Mopped my pop.

Not last night but the night before
Twenty-four robbers came knocking at my door.
As I ran OUT (jump out),
They ran IN (jump back in).
I asked them what they wanted
and this is what they said. . .

Spanish Dancer do the twist,
Spanish Dancer give a high kick,
Spanish Dancer turn around,
Spanish Dancer touch the ground,
Spanish Dancer get out of town!

Susie and Johnny sitting in a tree,
K-I-S-S-I-N-G
First comes love,
Then comes marriage,
Then comes Susie with a baby carriage

———

Jumping in groups of four or more
lets everyone take turns jumping in
and out of the rope. Here are
some rhymes that let you call in
the next jumper by their name:

Rickety, rickety blam!
My uncle's name is Sam.
He has a beard,
He's really weird.
He lets (kid's name) call him ma'am.

Rickety, rickety boo!
My sister's name is Sue.
She ate fried pork
With a knife and fork
And left the fat
For (kid's name).

Mother, mother,
I am ill,
Send for the doctor
Over the hill.
Send for the doctor,
Send for the nurse,
Send for the lady
With the alligator purse.

Ask me this,
And I'll tell you that.
Teacher, teacher,
Rat-tat-tat.
You sit in class
Upon your
Ask me this
And I'll tell you that.

SLAVES OF THE SPACE MUTANTS!

FREE-OLA!!

IN SPACE, WATER BOILS INSTANTLY.

This is a game for two teams: The Space Mutants vs. The Earthlings. First, boundaries are determined, like within the park, or a one-block area. The Space Mutants mark out a big circle, about 12 feet in diameter (White flour is a good thing to use for this). This is the launch pad. They then stand inside and count to 100. While they count, The Earthlings run and hide anywhere within the boundaries. The Space Mutants then go on a seek-and-capture mission, leaving one Mutant to guard the launch pad. When they find and tag an Earthling, the Earthling becomes enslaved and must go meekly into the launch pad. Any and all slaves can be freed to hide again if an Earthling can sneak up to the launch pad and run all the way through it shouting "FREE-OLA!" without getting captured. Play continues until all Earthlings are captured.

Ye Olde Treasure

START HERE. GO TO BIG TREE.

First, pick out a "treasure," and seal it in a shoebox. Then hide it somewhere in the yard or in the neighborhood. You may even want to *bury* the treasure.

Next, draw a few treasure maps like the one you see on this page. (A brown paper bag makes great map material!) Include clues and directions, such as where to start from, how many paces to walk, and which way to turn. . . but don't make it *too* easy. Clues are the most important part of this game. Don't be obvious. Be sneaky and indirect in leading people to the next spot!

Now, pass out the maps and see which one of your friends is clever enough to figure out your clues and find the treasure. And, don't forget, whoever finds it gets to keep it!

STOP

GO EAST. GO FETCH.

BIG TREE

LOOK AROUND AND MAKE A WISH.

"AHOY" WAS THE BATTLE-CRY OF THE NORSE AND DANISH VIKINGS WHEN THEY RUSHED THEIR GALLEYS UPON THE ENEMY.

HEAD SOUTH TILL YOU'RE ALL WASHED UP.

CARTOGRAPHIC THRILL-O-RAMA

Pick an area of your neighborhood to map out. It could be anything from the route you walk to school to your backyard. Count your steps between large objects that you'll want to draw on your map. Decide on the scale of your map. A good one to use is one inch = one yard (three feet). Draw a rough version with a pencil first to get everything where it should go. Once you've gotten it figured out, draw the final map using colored pencils or markers.

NOW, GO NORTH AND DON'T GO.

TAKE 14 PACES NORTH EAST.

Hunt

COUNT SIX POINTS DUE EAST.

COUNT 7 PACES SOUTH AND DIG.

PUT OUT A FIRE 30 PACES DUE SOUTH.

GO NORTH TO A DIVIDING LINE.

DIG HERE!

LOOK NORTH, I USED TO BE ALIVE.

Scavenger Hunt

Players divide into two or more teams of equal size.

Each team is given a list of about a dozen objects to find and bring back. Use your imagination to come up with things that you *can* find, but not right away, like a golf ball, a back issue of a certain magazine, a rock the size of a baseball, a pair of red socks, and a can of chunky tunafish packed in water.

Whichever team collects and brings back all the stuff on their list first, wins.

Springfield's SPLASH-A-RIFIC *Aquacade*

As if anyone needs to tell you how to stir up a wave when you've got access to a pool! But just in case you and your friends are feeling overcome by heat to the point that even your imaginations feel faint, here are a few suggestions. First, everyone should jump in with a big splash, and then...

WATER VOLLEYBALL

Stretch a volleyball or badminton net across the pool and split into two teams. Play volleyball like you normally would on land...only you're afloat! If one team is in the shallow end and one team is in the deep end, be sure to change sides after each team has served. This is much more strenuous than playing volleyball on land and will get you in great shape. And if you really like playing this game, join the lobby to make it an official Olympic sport!

Pool Basketball

Sometimes you can find floating basketball hoops for sale in the store. If not, rig up a basket on the deck at one or both ends of the pool and use that. The rules are the same as regular basketball only you can't dribble!

MARCO POLO

This game was created by the Chinese in the fifteenth century to make fun of how the Italian explorer Marco Polo was always getting lost on his journeys. He was so bad with directions, they teased, that he probably couldn't even follow the sound of his own name! It was so popular in the emperor's royal pools that now it's spread to every pool across America.

One person is chosen to be "It." "It" must close her eyes and count to thirty, then yell "Marco." All the other players in the pool answer, "Polo." Without opening her eyes, "It" tries to tag them by the sound of their voices. The other players try to get as near as possible to "It," but any time "It" says, "Marco," the other players must answer, no matter how dangerously close they may be. As soon as "It" tags someone, that player becomes "It." You can get out of the pool, but "It" can say, "Fish on dry land!" at any time, and anyone who is out of the water is automatically "It." If more than one player is out of the pool, the last one to jump back in is "It."

THE SEAHORSE SWIMS AT THE RATE OF ONE FOOT PER MINUTE.

D I V E S

JACKKNIFE

You must jump very high off the board for this dive. At the peak of the arc of the dive, bend forward and touch your toes, bending only at the waist and keeping your legs together and straight, like a real jackknife. As you descend, let your feet rise up behind you as your upper body reaches forward.

BACKDIVE

It takes a lot of courage and practice to master this dive. Stand at the edge of the pool facing away from the water. Place your hands together over your head and let yourself fall slowly backwards into the water, being sure to arch your back the whole way. You should enter the water hands first. If you've never done this before, ask a friend to help you by holding onto your waist and guiding you into the water. As you grow comfortable, try going off the low board . . . and then adding a little jump. It's fun!

SWAN DIVE

This is the most elegant of dives. Jump as high and far away from the board as you can. Keep your arms stretched far out from your sides at right angles to your body. Hold them there for the duration of the dive, bringing them together quickly and smoothly just as you enter the water. Always remember to keep your legs tightly together at the knees and ankles for best diving form. It helps to think graceful, birdlike thoughts while executing this dive.

CANNONBALL

The classic pool-draining, crowd-soaking, attention-getting splashy entrance! Mad at the world? This will make you feel better. Jump as high as you can off the board, tuck your legs, wrap your arms around your shins, and land on your butt in water. Style is not as important here as volume of water displaced.

CAN OPENER

If your cannonball didn't do the trick, this will. This granddaddy of all leaps is guaranteed to throw off more water than an Esther Williams spectacular!

LONDON BRIDGE

This game can be played by any number of players from two to twenty. Split into two teams and line up on the deck on either side of the pool. The first person in one line hits a beach ball over the pool to the first player on the other side. Without catching it, that person bats it back over the pool to the second player on the other side. The ball crosses back and forth over the pool (bridging the water, so to speak), with no player catching or holding the ball, just hitting it with their fingertips, making sure at the same time that the ball doesn't end up in the drink. But watch how often some players do!

SOME FOSSILS OF ALGAE ARE MORE THAN THREE BILLION YEARS OLD

Jump or Dive

One person is the caller; the others are divers. As each person approaches the end of the diving board in turn, they don't know whether they will be told to jump or dive. Only after they have left the board does the caller yell "Jump!" or "Dive!" See how many people end up doing bellyflops!

POOL TAG

One person is chosen to be "It." "It" tries to tag one of the other players who then becomes "It." A player can leave the water, but only for five seconds. If they stay out longer, they automatically become "It."

Treasure Diving

Throw a few things into the pool that will sink to the bottom. Then have everybody jump in and dive to find them. See who can collect the most in one breath.

UP PERISCOPE

This periscope allows you to spy on people, birds and animals completely undetected...maybe.

You will need:
☆ 2 one-quart milk cartons
☆ 2 mirrors, each about 1-7/8" by 2-7/8"
☆ masking tape

Cut the top off of one carton. Cut out a 1-1/2" area near the bottom, as shown. Tape over back of mirror so that if it breaks it will not shatter. Place mirror on a slant, in the lower back of carton. Adjust angle until you can see straight out the top of the carton when you look through the hole in the side. Tape mirror in place. (If the mirror is wider than the carton, cut slits in sides of carton.) This is one half of the periscope. To complete it, cut the top off another carton and repeat the same steps. Put the two cartons together with the top mirror facing away from you, squeezing the top of one carton so the other will slide down over and on top of it.
Paint camouflauge on it so no one will see you!

ONE-WAY TIME TRAVEL

Here is your chance at immortality. Leave behind a secret capsule with an image of yourself and your world for future generations to find. First, write down things like what you did this week, who you talked with on the phone, what TV shows you watched, what you studied in school, or who annoyed you the most and why. Be sure to be detailed in your explanations so that a stranger could really get a feel for what it's like to be you at this particular moment and place in time. Include some your favorite magazines, a snapshot of yourself in your favorite clothes, the menu from your school cafeteria, today's newspaper, etc. Put it all in a box, wrap the box in plastic, and bury it in a safe spot in the yard, or hide it in a remote part of the basement or attic, where no one will find it for a hundred years.

2x4 TITANIC

You can build this seaworthy craft in just a few minutes. And it runs under its own power!
You will need:
☆ a scrap block of wood – an end of an old 2x4 is perfect
☆ a plastic (not paper) milk carton
☆ 2 long nails
☆ rubber bands

Hammer nails into one end of wood block, just deep enough so they won't pull out and as wide apart as possible. Wrap a fat rubber band tautly around the nails. If you only have thin rubber bands, use two or three together. Cut a paddle from a milk carton that will fit easily between the nails and will stick out a little beyond them. Center the paddle between the rubber band, wind up the paddle, and launch your vessel!

TIME

Create a SUNDIAL

When you've been told to "go entertain yourself for an hour and don't come back inside before then," here's a good way to keep your folks honest. Most animals and plants use the sun to tell time, now you can too!

1. Cut a piece of wood or stiff cardboard about a foot square.

2. Use a compass to draw the largest circle possible on the square. Mark the center of the circle with a dot.

3. Drill a hole in the center and glue in a long, thin stick, or wooden dowel, perpendicular to the top of the wood block. If you're using cardboard, fasten a thin stick with lots of masking top so that it stands up straight.

4. Draw a line through the center of the circle. This will mark 12:00.

5. Attach the sundial to the top of a post and put it in a place that gets full sunlight (or lay the cardboard on a flat, sunny piece of ground) . Set it so the 12:00 mark points north, or at noon rotate sundial until the shadow of the pointer falls exactly on the 12:00 mark.

6. Each hour from 6:00 am to 6:00 pm, make a dot where the shadow hits the outside of the circle and label it with the time. Now you can tell the time simply by glancing at the sundial to see where the sun is casting its shadow.

THE SPLENDOR IN THE GRASS WHISTLE

(as dependable as the blues)

This is one of the oldest of all musical instruments — it even pre-dates the ukelele. Pluck a large sturdy blade of grass about three to four inches long (Fig. 1). Place it sideways (skinny edge of the blade towards you) between your thumbs, holding your hands as if you are clapping (Fig.2). Making sure the blade is taut between your thumbs, blow into the hollow created there. You should produce a high, shrill whistle, the natural frequency of which will send chills up a bird's (or parent's) back. So blow, baby, blow!

Fig. 1

Fig. 2

JIMBO'S J-9

SELF-INFLATED BOMBASTIC-ELASTIC BALLOON ROCKET

Use a little know-how and a lot of trial and error to harness the wild power of a runaway balloon!

You will need:

☆ a plastic drinking straw

☆ a long, straight balloon (not round)

☆ a rubber band

☆ a thin scrap of cardboard (postcards or manila folders are perfect)

Cut the straw in half, and push one piece inside the other. Now insert the straw a few inches into the balloon. Wrap a rubber band around the neck of the balloon to secure the straw. Make the stabilizer fin by cutting out a rectangular piece of thin cardboard from the postcard. Fold it in half and cut a notch in the middle of the folded edge just big enough to allow the straw to slip in snugly. Slip the stabilizer fin over the end of the straw just far enough so that it won't slip off. A small piece of tape will hold it in place.

You are now ready for a test launch. Blow up the balloon through the straw, aim it towards the stars, and let it go. If it zooms around too much, try a larger stabilizer fin. If it goes nowhere, go smaller. You can also adjust the thrust power by pinching the straw closed or opening it wider with a pencil. Blast off!

On the Road...

TWENTY QUESTIONS

A game for two or more players. One person thinks of a thing (try to be creative). All he tells the others is if it's animal, vegetable, or mineral. The other players take turns asking questions like, "Is it bigger than a skateboard?" or "Could you take it swimming?" The answerer can only say "yes" or "no," but he must tell the truth. If the mystery isn't solved in twenty questions, the answerer wins.

Another version is called "As Many Questions As It Takes." Think of *really* obscure things like "the piece of bubble gum I stuck to the underside of my desk in second grade." This game goes on until the answer is reached or you get to wherever you're going.

HIGHWAY ALPHABET

While you're driving along with nothing to do, look for letters of the alphabet in signs and license plates. You can play alone or make it a contest to see who can find all the letters first. Go through the alphabet in order. The easy way is that you can use any letter in the word. The harder way is that you can only use the first letter in the word. It can get tricky when you get to X or Z so you could agree at the beginning that you're gonna pass on those. Q is hard to find too.

The State Plate Search is kind of the same idea. Try to spot license plates from all fifty states. Good Luck!

Under My Bed

This game is best with a bunch of people. One person starts by saying, "I looked under my bed and I found an aardvark" (or something else that starts with the letter "A"). The next person says, "I looked under my bed and I found an aardvark and a basketball" (or something starting with the letter "B"). Continue adding objects to the list in alphabetical order.

THE WORLD'S 500 MILLION CARS, TRUCKS, AND BUSES ACCOUNT FOR MORE AIR POLLUTION THAN ANY OTHER HUMAN ACTIVITY.

BART'S RHYMING DICTIONARY
"I'm a poet, and don't I know it!"

You can be a rhymin', two-timin', tree climbin' Simple Simon, too. Here are some words that rhyme. See how many songs or poems you can make with them. Then try some rhymes of your own.

underachiever	receiver	fever	
deceiver	cleaver	believer	
retriever	weaver	leave her	

EXAMPLE:
What? You don't do the rhumba?!
Aye, carumba! Sorry, wrong number!

Or try a combination of rhymes:

fly	by	lie
pie	sigh	die
high	guy	necktie
sky	my	why

cheese	sleaze	please
disease	ease	tease
knees	wheeze	sneeze
breeze	geez!	fleas

EXAMPLE:
This is the fly
That buzzes by
And spreads diseases
Wherever it pleases.

IN 1989 AMERICAN MOTOR VEHICLES TRAVELED 2.09 TRILLION VEHICLE MILES; ENOUGH TO MAKE ABOUT 380 ROUND TRIPS TO THE PLANET NEPTUNE.

EVERY FIFTEEN DEGREES OF LONGITUDE IS EQUAL TO THE DISTANCE TRAVELED IN AN HOUR OF THE EARTH'S ROTATION.

GOOFY PLACES TO VISIT

When it comes time to pick the destination of your family vacation, try talking your folks into going someplace even weirder than Aunt Selma's. It could be a giant bowling pin or a building in the shape of a dinosaur. It could be someplace that offers bizarre entertainment like alligator wrestling. Now these places aren't usually listed by the Automobile Association of America so it will take some investigating to find the ones in your area. Here are a few to get you started.

FLINTSTONE'S BEDROCK CITY in Valle, AZ and BEDROCK CITY in Custer, SD

STORYBOOK FOREST in Ligonier, PA

WORLD'S LARGEST BUG in Colorado Springs, CO

ST. AUGUSTINE ALLIGATOR FARM in St. Augustine, FL

WORLD'S LARGEST TIRE in Dearborn, MI

TUPPERWARE MUSEUM in Kissimmee, FL

ROCK CITY & RUBY FALLS in Lookout Mountain, GA/TN

GARDEN OF EDEN in Lucas, KS

WORLD'S LARGEST TWINE BALL in Darwin, MN

TALKING ROCKS CAVERNS in Branson, MO

NATIONAL ATOMIC MUSEUM in Albuquerque, NM

WORLD'S LARGEST SIX PACK in La Crosse, WI

THE OREGON VORTEX in Gold Hill, OR

AMERICAN MUSEUM OF ATOMIC ENERGY in Oak Ridge, TN

LAND OF KONG in Eureka Springs, AR

PREHISTORIC GARDEN in Port Orford, OR

GRACELAND (of course) in Memphis, TN

80,000 SQUARE MILES, AN AREA THE SIZE OF KANSAS, TURNS TO DESERT ANNUALLY.

HAWAII IS MOVING TOWARD JAPAN AT A RATE OF 3 INCHES A YEAR WHILE NORTH AMERICA AND EUROPE ARE MOVING APART ABOUT 1 INCH PER YEAR.

ONLY ABOUT 30% OF THE WORLD'S LAND IS INHABITED AND ABOUT 15% IS TRULY NATURAL LANDSCAPE.

ROADSIDE OR MAGAZINE SCAVENGER HUNT

Here's a good way to waste time when you're stuck in the car. Start by making a list of items to look for. (The more specific the better, like a green baseball cap or a pink pick-up truck with a dog in the back.) Now start searching and keep track of the items you find. You can either look in magazines or out the window. The first person to find them all wins. What they win we don't exactly know.

READING MAPS

I know. You're thinking, "How boring!" But actually it can be fairly amusing to look at the map of the area you're traveling through. Or even areas you aren't traveling through. Some of the names of towns can be pretty hilarious. And you might find some places you'd like to stop and visit. It can be fun to track your progress along the road as you pass each city. You can annoy your parents by showing them where you are when they get lost.

ANNOYING CAR SONGS

If you don't like these songs, make up your own words to songs you know or try singing the words of one song to the tune of another.

To the tune of "The Caissons Go Rolling Along"
OVER HILL OVER DALE WE HAVE BUSTED OUT OF JAIL,
AND THE COPPERS ARE HOT ON OUR TRAIL.
THEY'VE BROUGHT GUNS THEY'VE BROUGHT KNIVES,
THEY HAVE EVEN BROUGHT THEIR WIVES.
OH THE COPPERS ARE HOT ON OUR TRAIL.
SO IT'S HI HI HEE
TO THE PENITENTIARY
CALL OUT YOUR NUMBERS LOUD AND CLEAR!
(SHOUT) THREE BEERS!
FOR WHERE 'ERE WE GO,
YOU WILL ALWAYS KNOW
THAT THE COPPERS ARE HOT ON OUR TRAIL.

To the tune of "On Top of Old Smokey"
ON TOP OF SPAGHETTI
ALL COVERED WITH CHEESE
I LOST MY POOR MEATBALL
WHEN SOMEBODY SNEEZED.

IT ROLLED OFF THE TABLE
AND ONTO THE FLOOR
AND THEN MY POOR MEATBALL
ROLLED OUT OF THE DOOR.

IT ROLLED IN THE GARDEN
AND UNDER A BUSH
AND THEN MY POOR MEATBALL
WAS NOTHING BUT MUSH.

SO IF YOU EAT SPAGHETTI
ALL COVERED WITH CHEESE
HANG ONTO YOUR MEATBALL
AND DON'T EVER SNEEZE.

The whole point of this song is to sing the cock-a-doodle-doo part as loud and high as you can.

I HAVE A ROOSTER, MY ROOSTER LOVES ME.
I FEED MY ROOSTER ON GREEN BAY TEA.
MY LITTLE ROOSTER GOES COCK-A-DOODLE-
    DOODLE-DOODLE-DOODLE-DOODLE-DO!

I HAVE A DINOSAUR, MY DINOSAUR LOVES ME.
I FEED MY DINOSAUR ON GREEN BAY TEA.
MY LITTLE DINOSAUR GOES ROAR, ROAR, ROAR!
MY LITTLE ROOSTER GOES COCK-A-DOODLE-
    DOODLE-DOODLE-DOODLE-DOODLE-DO!
Continue to add animals until your folks scream for mercy.

To the tune of "Alouette"
ALL YOU ET-A
THINK OF ALL YOU ET-A
ALL YOU ET-A
THINK OF ALL YOU ET
THINK OF ALL THE PIE YOU ET
THINK OF ALL THE PIE YOU ET
PIE YOU ET, PIE YOU ET.
OO-OO-OO-OH
Repeat and add foods indefinitely.

And don't forget the classic:
99 BOTTLES OF BEER
    ON THE WALL
99 BOTTLES OF BEER
TAKE ONE DOWN
PASS IT AROUND
98 BOTTLES OF BEER
    ON THE WALL
Continue counting backward till you reach one bottle.

MOUNT WAIALEALE IN HAWAII IS THE WETTEST PLACE ON EARTH WITH AN AVERAGE RAINFALL OF 472 INCHES A YEAR.

BOTTOMLESS PIT

GET YOUR PHOTO

THINGS TO TAKE ALONG

Whether you're camping in your backyard or the deep woods, don't leave home without:

☆ A flashlight. Invaluable when nature calls in the middle of the night!

☆ Extra batteries and bulbs. Just because the flashlight worked last year doesn't mean it works this year.

☆ A compass. You never know when the rest of your party will decide to get lost.

☆ A poncho. If it doesn't rain, you can sit on it.

☆ A toothbrush. You are still in social contact with others.

☆ Matches. Used properly, you'll be able to start a fire for cooking or storytelling.

☆ Utensils. You can eat your food with your fingers but who wants to?

☆ A sleeping bag. Ssssh! Be careful not to wake it!

☆ A canteen. When filled with water, it's the essential thirst aid kit.

☆ A watch. You'll know at exactly what time you started hearing those weird noises.

☆ A ghost story. Look ahead 6 pages for tips.

☆ A whoopee cushion. Transform your sleeping bag into a barrel of laffs!

☆ Junk food. It's a scientific fact: if eaten in the Great Outdoors, it's not bad for you.

GIMME SHELTER

Everyone needs to feel protected.
A classic tent can be made from a few items:
- A large blanket, tarp, or sheet of strong plastic
- String, twine, or rope (about 15 ft. – a clothesline works really well)
- A few clothespins
- Rocks or wooden stakes

Tie the rope or string between two trees or anything that will keep it about three to four feet off the ground. Drape the blanket or tarp over the string and secure it with clothespins. Anchor the blanket to the ground with rocks or stakes (but don't use stakes on one of your mom's good blankets!). You can spread another tarp on the ground inside for a floor, and close one end with more clothespins for more privacy.

For indoor campers, make a tent by draping a blanket between chair backs or over tables, using clothespins to close any open ends.

THE WINDS OF A TORNADO MAY REACH SPEEDS UP TO 300 M.P.H.

THIS WAY **GO LEFT** **GO RIGHT** **WATCH OUT! DANGER!** **WE'RE STARVING! HELP!**

Totally Secret-Coded Trail Signs

If you're out on the trail and you want only your good friends to find you, take a tip from the native Americans and use these handy trail signs.

BIRD WATCHING

There are hundreds of different kinds of birds up there in the sky. We'd like to tell you all about them, but that would take a whole other book. How many can you identify? Use binoculars and a notebook to keep track. (Look out for pigeons!)

PIGEONS ARE REALLY JUST RATS WITH WINGS.

Tracking the Wild Beasties

Look for animal tracks in the dirt or mud and follow them. If you're at the shore, bird tracks in the sand are also easy to follow. You can find specific patterns to identify in the library. Cats and dogs are easy to follow, but be careful of really large prints . . . it might be Big Foot!

LEAN-TO HOW-TO'S

For hot summer nights when better air circulation is needed, a lean-to may be more comfortable than a tent. Tie your string up higher or rig up two tall posts with a crossbeam to attach your blanket to. Secure it with clothespins or nails. Pull the blanket out to form a triangle-shaped inside and anchor it with rocks to the ground. If you are backyard-camping, you can nail a blanket to the side of your garage, if your dad says it's OK. If you can, try to position it so the blanket blocks the morning sun so you can sleep late. And be sure to wear plenty of mosquito repellent!

GONE FISHIN'

Fishing is great fun if you love sitting in one spot doing nothing for long periods of time. So if patience is your virtue, you'll need a fishing pole. For the simplest version, tie a safety pin (opened) to one end of a string, and tie the other to the end of a long, thin stick. Real fishing line is the best string to use. Drop a rock tied to a separate string to gauge the distance to the bottom of your fishing hole (FIG. A). Tie a short, fat stick on your fishing line as a bobber, so your hook dangles about eight inches up from the bottom (FIG. B). Worms, grasshoppers, crickets, roaches, cheese, stale bread, or even marshmallows make good bait. Toss your baited line gently into the water, lean back against a shady tree...and wait. And don't be greedy. Only catch as much as you intend to eat.

FIG. A   FIG. B

OUT ON A LIMB

Thirty percent of the earth's land surface is covered by forests, so it might be helpful to know a little about them. Trees can be categorized in different ways. One way is by the nature of their leaves – either broadleaf or needleleaf. Most needleleaf trees are cone-bearing, or coniferous, as well. Another way to categorize trees is by how often they lose and grow leaves. Trees that are leafless for a season are deciduous trees; those that shed and replace some leaves while remaining green all year are called evergreen trees. But the most important category to know is climbing trees. Look for trees with big, thick branches that grow close together with the lowest one close enough to the ground so you can reach it.

EVERGREEN

OAK

CYPRESS

MAKE-A-BIG-MESS LEAF PRINTING

Here's what you'll need:
- white glue
- tree leaves
- cardboard
- poster paint
- paintbrush
- white drawing paper

THE TOTAL NUMBER OF ORGANISMS IN ONE KILOGRAM OF SOIL IS LIKELY TO EXCEED A HUNDRED BILLION.

Apply glue to the top of a leaf (the smooth side) and glue it to a piece of cardboard to dry. "Ink" the leaf by painting a thin coat of paint on it. Place a piece of white paper over the inked side of the leaf, press gently, and carefully pull it up. Repeat the process or apply other leaf prints in different colors for various design effects. If you don't have any cardboard, try placing the painted leaf face-down on the paper, then covering it with a piece of newspaper and carefully rolling over it with a rolling pin orsmooth-sided bottle.

MAKE-NOT-QUITE-AS-BIG-A-MESS LEAF RUBBINGS

For a simpler and less messy form of leaf printing, use crayons instead of paint. Place the leaf or leaves rough side up under a piece of thin white drawing paper. Remove the paper wrapping from a crayon and rub it sideways on the paper over the leaf. The leaf pattern will appear on the paper. Experiment with various color combinations.

SLOPPY SPLATTER LEAF PRINTS

This is an ideal way to be a pig and not get into trouble. Cover a large surface with newspaper before you begin this one, and keep a rag nearby for your hands. Arrange differently-shaped leaves on a piece of white paper to make a nice pattern. Dip an old toothbrush into thinned down poster paint or watercolors. Let the excess paint drip off into the container, then point the toothbrush at the leaves and drag your thumb across the bristles towards you, splattering the paint around the leaves. Splattering on the wall or nearby chintz furniture may be hazardous to your future artistic career! Wipe your thumb off before using another color. Carefully lift the leaves to reveal stunning stencil patterns.

ELM

MAPLE (In Fall)

NEVERGREEN

MOOSEBARK MAPLE

PAPERBARK MAPLE

ELM

COMMON ASH

SUGAR MAPLE

CAUCASIAN OAK

THOROUGHLY SMASHED FLOWERS BOOKMARK

You can press any objects – flower blossoms, leaves, ferns, grasses – as long as they're not too fat. They also need to be fresh but not wet. Press the plants you choose between two pieces of white paper in the pages of a thick book for a couple of weeks, until they have dried completely. Arrange your dried plants on a heavy piece of paper, about 2 1/2" x 8". Use just a spot of glue to keep them in place. Let dry. Cover the entire bookmark with a slightly larger piece of clear contact paper, laying it over the leaves. Starting at one end, rub your fingers over the contact paper as you lower it to press out any air bubbles. Trim the excess contact paper from the edge of the bookmark.

STUMP SLEUTHING

First find a tree stump. Count the number of rings to see how old this particular tree was when it was cut down. Each of the rings indicates a year. The narrow rings indicate difficult years—maybe there was a drought or some insects had infested it. Or it could mean that it was crowded out by bigger trees. The wider rings show a good year with plenty of rain and sunshine. You might be able to see where a fire caused damage and how the tree healed itself over the years.

A TREE IS BORN.

SOMETHING WAS LEANING ON THE TREE SO IT GREW MORE ON ONE SIDE TO HELP SUPPORT ITSELF.

A FOREST FIRE HURT THE TREE HERE.

NARROW RINGS COULD MEAN A DROUGHT OR INSECT DAMAGE.

THE HEALTHY YEARS. THE RINGS ARE FURTHER APART.

SEMI-SECRET SEMAPHORES

Need to send a secret message? Try this method that Patty & Selma picked up from a tattooed sailor in Macao. Make these signal flags, or just use your arms. For breaks between words, hold both arms down in front of you.

 A

 B

 C

 D

 E

 F

 G

 H

 I

 J

K

HOW TO BUILD A CAMPFIRE
NUMBER ONE RULE OF THE WILDS:
ALWAYS HAVE ADULT SUPERVISION WHENEVER USING FIRE.

Be sure to find out what the fire rules are in the area you'll be camping in. You may need to obtain a fire permit. This includes your backyard! Don't build a fire on a breezy night; sparks can fly up into the trees and set them a blaze.

Once you have the permit, dig a shallow hole in the ground about two feet in diameter, and surround it with rocks. Clear an area about fifteen feet in all directions around the hole, removing any dry leaves or other flammable materials. You can use those dry leaves and small twigs as kindling, or you can use crumpled up newspaper. Place a pile of it at the bottom of your hole. Put small branches in the form of a teepee on top of your kindling, and light the kindling. Keep it lit by blowing on it or gently waving a piece of cardboard over the embers. Carefully add larger pieces of wood, making sure not to smother the flames. Within minutes you should have a nice cozy fire going.

Putting out your fire correctly is as important as starting it. Even if the embers seem dead, stir them with a stick, pour water all over the pit, and stir again. Make sure every spark is gone, and that the ashes are absolutely cold before leaving the area.

TURKEY LEADS THE WORLD IN CEREAL CONSUMPTION

MARGE'S PERFECT PANCAKES

Mix together:
1 egg, beaten
1 cup buttermilk
1/4 cup salad oil

Sift together:
1 cup flour
1 tsp baking powder
1/2 tsp baking soda
1 Tbl sugar
1/2 tsp salt

Mix together wet and dry ingredients. Melt a little bit of butter or oil in a hot skillet. A cast iron one works the best. Pour spoonfuls of the batter into the pan forming small circles. Don't put them too close together or it will be hard to turn them over. When the batter is full of bubbles, carefully turn each pancake over with a spatula. They're ready when both sides are golden brown. Slap them on a plate, add butter and maple syrup, and gobble them up.

BACON 'N' EGGS

One of the best smells in the whole world is bacon cooking on a campfire as the sun comes up on a beautiful morning. So just slap some on a cast iron skillet, browning it on both sides. When it's done, fry a couple of eggs in the fat that's left in the pan.

THERE ARE USUALLY NO MORE THAT SIX LINKS IN A FOOD CHAIN

CLASSIC MARSHMALLOW ROASTING:

Find a straight stick that's long enough to reach over the fire without burning your hands. You can also use a straightened coathanger. Poke it through the marshmallow (use the big ones) and hang it over the fire, turning as it browns. When it's toasted to your liking, pull it off and eat it while it's hot.

SIMPSONS SUN TEA

Find a large jar with a screw-top lid. Make sure it doesn't leak when turned upside down. Fill it with fresh, cold water. Put a handful of your favorite teabags inside, leaving the strings hanging over the edge of the jar. Screw the lid on tightly, trapping the strings. Turn the jar upside down and place in strong, direct sunlight for two hours. Squeeze fresh lemon juice into it and voila. . . delicious, naturally-brewed tea.

S'MORES: MESSY MOLTEN MARSHMALLOW MADNESS

Once you've mastered the art of roasting marshmallows, it's time to graduate to the ultimate delicacy of campfire cooking! Girl Scouts and ex-Girl Scouts are the unsurpassed masters of the fine art of making S'mores. Try to find one to show you how. If you're on your own, here's the basic recipe:

Place four squares of a chocolate bar on one-half of a Graham cracker. Toast a marshmallow over a fire and place it on top of the chocolate. Put the other half of the Graham cracker on top of the marshmallow (like the top piece of bread on a sandwich). Open your mouth extra wide and bite down on the most delicious thing that will ever enter it! When you finish that one, you'll want s'more!

AMERICANS EAT 11 BILLION SLICES OF PIZZA EACH YEAR.

OATMEAL BOX

BART & LISA'S SOLAR-POWERED HOT DIGGITY DOG ROASTER

This device works best on a bright, sunny day, which means that if you live in Seattle you'll only get to use it three days out of the year. Here's how it works: Cut the sides out of an oatmeal box as shown above, and cover the entire inside surface with aluminum foil. Straighten out a wire coathanger and poke it through one end of the box, then through the hotdog, then through the other end. Set it out in a sunny spot, and turn it like a rotisserie. It will take a few minutes, but will taste extra good, and it conserves energy by using readily available sunrays!

COCOA, OR CHOCOLATE, WAS A FAVORITE DRINK OF THE AZTECS.

DO-IT-YOURSELF PAPER CUP

Fig. 1
Fig. 2
Fig. 3
Fig. 4
Fig. 5

Fold a square piece of paper in half diagonally (fig. 1). With the point up, fold over the right flap (fig. 2), and then the left flap (fig. 3). Turn down the top flaps on each side (fig. 4), and open your cup (fig. 5).

L M N O P Q R S T U V W X Y Z

Nighttime is the best time to do most of your stargazing. The sun hogs all the attention during the day. So wait for a dark, clear night with no moon and pick a spot away from other distracting lights. Lie on your back and look upwards, let your eyes adjust, and see how many stars and constellations you can spot and name.

TOTALLY TWINKLY TIN CAN LANTERN

This is a great way to illuminate the night while camping or just hanging out in your backyard. Find a can with a smooth surface and remove the label by peeling or soaking it off. Draw a pattern of dots on the outside of the can with a felt marker. Fill the can with water and place it the freezer for 24 hours. Remove the can from the freezer and place it on its side on a towel. Use assorted nails to pierce through the pattern of dots you've drawn.

Hammer the nails in just far enough to pierce the metal. The ice will help the can retain its shape while you're pounding it.

Hammer two holes for a handle on either side of the top of the can.

Put a candle in the bottom, and attach a piece of wire through your top holes as a handle. Light the candle and enjoy your display!

Polaris, the North Star is also known by sailors as the "lodestar." The Navajo Indians call it "The Star That Does Not Move." This star stays constant, and unlike other stars remains visible the entire year. All the other stars in the sky rotate around it. Sailors and travelers have used it for centuries to tell which direction is North. Polaris is the last star that forms the tip of the Little Dipper constellation.

NORTH STAR

Start with the most familiar – the Big Dipper. The two stars that form the front of the cup point to the star named Polaris – the North Star.

BIG DIPPER

The planet Venus is visible just after sunset. It's the brightest object in the sky besides the moon and certain UFOs.

VENUS

Mars has a steady, red light.

MARS

SHOOTING STAR

In winter months, look for Orion, the hunter. He is easily distinguished by the three bright stars of his belt. At his shoulder is the bright star named Betelgeuse. Some say movie director Tim Burton comes from this star.

Betelgeuse

ORION

Get a star guide from the library to help you find these stars and others. Impress your friends with your knowledge!

EACH GALAXY CONTAINS ABOUT 1,000 MILLION STARS.

SPOOKY GHOST STORY TIPS

You gotta wait till it gets really dark to tell a ghost story. And it's gotta be a scary one. Here's some special effects to add to the mood:

☆ Hold a flashlight up to your chin so the light shines upwards over your face. This creates really weird shadows and makes you look kind of creepy.

☆ Have a friend secretly assist you. As you tell the story, your friend sits quietly in the group. And then, just at the right moment, when the story is at its most nerve-wracking point, your friend jumps up and lets out the most blood-curdling scream imaginable. A real crowd-pleaser!

☆ And, if you're not into ghosts, you can tell equally ghastly and alarming stories about space mutants or psycho-killers or giant, murderous insects or thundery politicians. The main thing is that you scare the hoo-hah outta everybody.

NATURE'S FLYING FLASHLIGHTS

In many parts of the country summertime means firefly time. These glowing insects come out at dusk. If you're quick on your feet, you can catch them. Put them in a jar for observation (punch small holes in the top first). Be sure to let them go free before you go inside for the night.

Way back, years ago, Springfield had this huge insane asylum for the _stupid_ and _greasy_ way out on the edge of town. It was a big, _sweaty_ looking building, and just driving past it made you feel all _____ and _____. Well, one night this _____ dude and his _____ babe were parked just down the road at the local lover's lane. They were sittin' in the _____ glow of the nuclear power plant, listening to the radio and hugging and smooching and acting all _____ and _____ like young dudes and babes do. And then, all of a sudden, this _____ announcer comes on the radio with a special bulletin: "Flash! Mad Dog Morrison, the notoriously _____ one-armed psycho-killer has just escaped from the Springfield Insane Asylum! Mad Dog has a big hook in place of his right hand and is considered _____ and _____! Springfield citizens are advised to stay inside and bolt the doors!" Well, man. The babe totally freaks! She gets all _____ and _____ and tells the dude to take her home right away. So, like, he starts the car and as they drive off they hear this horribly _____ scream like, "EEEEEEAAAAAAARRRRRGGGGHHHHH!!!" So, whoa! This really gets them all _____ and _____! They tear outta there back to the babe's house behind the Kwik-E Mart! The dude jumps outta the car and runs around to open the babe's door and just as he reaches for the door, he sees it! He sees what caused that awful _____ and _____ scream they heard. There! On the handle of the car door was the severed hook of Mad Dog Morrison. . . ripped from its socket just as the _____ maniac was about to open the door!

A GIBBOUS MOON IS A MOON THAT IS ROUNDED BUT NOT FULL.

THE EARTH ORBITS THE SUN AT 1,120 MILES PER MINUTE.

OTTO'S WEIRD TALE

Write each description from the list on a 3 x5 index card and deal the cards out to all the players. The narrator reads Otto's Weird Tale, pausing at the blanks. In turn, each player reads a card to fill in the missing words.

nervous

silly

excitable

slack-jawed

deranged

cheesey

unhinged

puffed up

high strung

smug-faced

itchy

fool-brained

insufferable

feeble-minded

squinty-eyed

overwrought

stupid

greasy

incoherent

scratchy

giddy

squeamish

fussy

sweaty

bewildered

THE EARLY NATIVE AMERICANS LIVED THEIR WHOLE LIVES OUTSIDE IN HARMONY WITH THEIR SURROUNDINGS. THAT'S WHY THEY HAD SUCH A DEEP UNDERSTANDING OF OUR PLACE IN THE GREAT SCHEME OF THINGS. MAYBE WE COULD LEARN SOMETHING FROM THEM AND HAVE SOME FUN TOO.

SEED NECKLACE

From cavemen to hippies, people have always adorned themselves with necklaces. Instead of swallowing all those watermelon seeds and growing plants in your belly, try wearing them around your neck. Use a needle and thread to string different types of seeds together. Use food coloring to dye them different colors!

BEADED BASEBALL CAP

You can buy beads from a craft or hobby store. Poke a threaded needle from the underside of your cap to where you want to start on the brim. String six beads and lay them in place, then run the needle down into the cap and bring it back up through to start the next row. Continue sewing in this way until you have finished the cap. Use the same number of beads per line and vary the color to create a design.

HEADBAND

The most basic wardrobe element of almost every tribe in North America, headbands can be very fancy or plain. Cut a strip of leather, cloth or construction paper the size of your head or larger, and staple, tape, glue or sew it closed. Decorate it with colorful patterns, and cut two little slits in the back to pass a feather through. You're all set!

TRIBAL SHIRTS AND DRESSES

Find a T-shirt the appropriate size that you can cut up and decorate (use a larger and longer one for the dress). Using scissors, cut 12" of fringe at the bottom and at the sleeves, the thinner the better. Decorate it with beads (sewn or glued on) and strips of colored cloth or leather, and paint a design to signify what tribe you want it to represent.

NATIVE AMERICAN FACE PAINTING

Most of the face painting of the Native Americans wasn't for war. It was a way to protect themselves from the weather and bug bites. It also was a way to show rank within the tribe and was used for many religious ceremonies. Here are just a few designs from various tribes. Try 'em on your self using face paint. Or design your own!

| KANSAS | ASSINIBOINS | PLAINS CREE | CHEYENNE | PLAINS CREE | BLACKFEET |
| SIOUX-TETON DAKOTA | BLACKFEET | PAWNEE | KIOWA | CHEYENNE | MANDANS |

Today's Project in... FLANDERS' GARAGE

WHERE EVERYTHING IS PEACHY-KEEN, SPICK 'N' SPAN, AND *IN ITS PLACE*, BY GOLLY!

Hi there, young people! You know, there's nothing quite like that special satisfaction we do-it-yourselfers get when we do-it-ourselves! Just try your hand at one of these easy-to-make birdfeeders, and soon you'll be making nifty things of your own original design.   Happy Hammering!

Ned Flanders

LET'S FEED THOSE PESKY BIRDS!

THE NATURAL

The most inconspicuous feeder of them all. Spoon peanut butter between the petals of a pine cone, then roll it in birdseed and hang.

THE JAVA JOINT

Cut the top and bottom out of an empty coffee can. Put plastic lids on both ends and cut a hole in each. Slide a stick through the plastic for a perch.

THE LAZY BOYD
Your feathered friends will love the unhindered access to this one – it's just a piece of plywood or a board supported by a stump or a 4" x 4" piece of wood. Cats love this one too!

IN A PICKLE

Wrap an old pickle jar with cloth or chicken wire (wash it out first!). Hang it from a string in a tree.

THE COCO BOWL

Not a football game, but coconut shell sawed in half, hollowed out, and hung with strings.

THE CHINESE THEATER

String up two wooden or plastic bowls, holding them in place with a couple of knots.

THE BLEACH JOB

Rinse out a bleach or other plastic container, cut a window in it, and suspend it from its own handle.

> A BIRD'S FEATHERS CAN WEIGH UP TO TWICE AS MUCH AS ITS SKELETON.

THE CALCIUM DEPOSIT

Yep, an old milk carton with a branch stuck through it and a hole cut out.

ALTERNATIVE PROJECT!

LITTLE TODD'S TERRARIUM

Here's a handy little project that utilizes that old goldfish bowl that's been cluttering up the storage shelves the past few seasons. If it's already been thrown out, a large glass jar with a screw top lid will do just dandy.
In addition, you'll need:
- gravel (enough to cover the bowl's floor)
- charcoal (same amount)
- terrarium soil (store-bought, or mix 1 cup sterilized potting soil, 2/3 cup perlite and 1/3 cup peat moss)
- small plants (ferns, violets, wild strawberry, matted mosses)
- mister or spray bottle with water

Clean and dry your container. Spoon 3/4" gravel into the bottom for drainage. To absorb odors, sprinkle in enough charcoal to cover gravel. Spoon in 2 inches of soil, then add your plants, spreading the roots out horizontally. Cover with more soil and tap it down. Mist the plants and put the lid on. (If you're using a goldfish bowl, use a glass dish or plastic film to seal it.) Your terrarium should now be self-sustaining.

After a week, if you see excess condensation on the inside of the glass, remove the lid for a little while.

Bless This Mess!

MR. FIX IT

Knarly Knots

THE FISHERMAN'S BEND

This is great for tying a rope to a tree branch, but make sure both are plenty strong before taking your first swing.

BOWLINE

Another good hitching knot. You can pull and pull on this knot as hard as you want, and still untie it readily by unthreading the loop, which will move easily. This is how novice sailors are taught to tie the bowline (a classic sailor's knot): "The rabbit goes out the hole, around the tree, and down back into the hole again."

LASSO

Here is the classic cowboy knot of yore. Practice first on inanimate objects (an upside down chair is good) before you try for moving targets. Hitch your rope to a wild steer — or older brother.

ACTUAL USES!

FISHERMAN'S BENDS

A TIRE SWING!
Use your new-found skill to create a neighborhood attraction...and charge admission!

← BOWLINES →

HOMEMADE RINGS!
Use cut pieces of an old garden hose for handles and create your own outdoor gymnasium!

CAPTURE A BULLY!
Be a hero! Make the neighborhood safe for everyone!

LASSO KNOT

RADICAL ROPE LADDER

Even if you don't have a treehouse, you can make this ladder and keep it under your bed for emergency escapes. It's made of wooden rungs held in place with a simple hitch knot (with an extra safety loop in the knot).

fig. 1

Use wooden dowling the thickness of a broom handle and 18" long for each rung. Allow twelve inches between rungs, and figure out how many you will need to make the right length ladder.

Cut two equal lengths of rope. Take one and, leaving eighteen inches hanging free below the bottom rung, make your first knot onto the rung (see fig. 1). Take the rope up the front of the rung, over the top, and down the back. Make a loop round to the front, pass the rope through the loop, and pull it tight. Make the knot three inches in from the end of the rung.

After leaving twelve inches between rungs, make the knot again onto the second rung, and so on until you reach the top. The other side of the ladder is knotted in the same way. Make sure the rungs are level and never forget the little safety loop in each knot.

MAKE A MONKEY SWING

You'll be scratchin' and screamin' when you ride on this swing! You'll need a piece of 3/4" plywood cut to about one foot in diameter. Drill a hole in the middle just thick enough to slip a piece of strong rope through. Tie a huge knot in the bottom of the rope and tie the other end to a thick, secure branch of a tree. Now go ape!

BUILD BART'S HIGH-RISE HIDE-OUT

If you're lucky enough to have a big tree that's got a sturdy limb and open space (to say nothing of really cool parents who will let you build a treehouse), then you're ahead of most of us. And if you have someone to help you build it, then you're sittin' pretty. But if you can't make one up in a tree, you can still have a great clubhouse right here on terra firma. Find a big bush with space under the branches, and build walls and doors with other branches, cardboard, sheets and blankets, or even rocks. Or latch onto a huge cardboard box, like the kind refrigerators come in, and stow it in a hard-to-spot place behind the house. You can even make one with old pieces of wood just like you would with a real treehouse. The important thing is to fill it with all kinds of cool stuff. Pick a secret password that only you and your closest friends know.

ESSENTIAL CLUBHOUSE SUPPLIES

Water balloons – an absolute must for any treehouse arsenal.
Comic books – the preferred reading material of thousands.
Slingshot – don't put out an eye!
Binoculars – there are few better vantage points in any neighborhood.
Magnifying glass – great for punishing invading ants and bugs.
Junk food – do we need to explain why?

The CASE of the MISSING CASE

It was a typical Thursday afternoon at Moe's Tavern. Homer and Sam were drinking beer and watching the Monster Truck Rally on TV. Larry was shooting pool and some guy down at the end of the bar was reading a sleazy tabloid. Moe was bringing up three cases of Duff beer from the storeroom when the phone rang. Moe went around the bar to answer it, but it was just some crank asking if his refrigerator was running.

As Moe hung up the phone he noticed three things right away: Police Chief Wiggum had just come into the tavern, Ned Flanders was jogging by outside, and one case of Duff beer was missing.

"Hey!" yelled Moe. "What's going on around here?!"

Can you find the clues and let poor Moe know what's going around here?

1. Could Homer have taken the case of Duff?

2. Could Sam have taken the case of Duff?

3. Could Larry have taken the case of Duff?

4. Could Ned Flanders have taken the case of Duff?

5. Could Police Chief Wiggum have taken the case of Duff?

6. Could the guy reading the paper have taken the case of Duff?

7. Is the case of Duff still in Moe's tavern?

8. If so, do you see any clues as to who might have moved it?

9. Do you think this was the work of a criminal mind or just a practical joker?

Answers in back of book.

WHITE WATER WIPEOUT!

Splash! It looks like a typical Simpsons vacation. Hidden in this picture are
24 items that went overboard along with Homer. Can you spot 'em?

Answer in back of book.

Cornered!!

Bart is trapped in the corner of his room, and it's almost time for *The Krusty the Clown Show* on TV. Can you help him find a path that doesn't cross over any of the objects scattered on the bed and the floor?

Answer in back of book.

Get The Lead Out

SAY WHAT?!

1C		2B	3E	4B	5D	6E	7A		8D	9A	10E	11B
12A	13D		14A	15B	16D		17B	18B	19E	20C	21B	22D

Answer each of the questions below. The first letter of each word will spell out the name of the person who is being quoted. Then enter the letters into the boxes above according to the numbers and solve the quotation.

A. Famous whale's first name.

‾12‾ ‾9‾ ‾14‾ ‾7‾

B. Mindless person; no-brainer.

‾4‾ ‾15‾ ‾2‾ ‾17‾ ‾11‾ ‾18‾ ‾21‾

C. Initials of the smallest state in the USA

‾20‾ ‾1‾

D. Gosh! Gee!

‾16‾ ‾22‾ ‾5‾ ‾8‾ ‾13‾

E. Very bad; wicked.

‾3‾ ‾10‾ ‾19‾ ‾6‾

THERE ARE 201 DIFFERENT MAIN LANGUAGES SPOKEN ON EARTH AND ALMOST 100 DIFFERENT KINDS OF SCRIPT.

Answers in back of book.

MARGE'S MIXED-UP JUMBLE

PAPER WAS INVENTED IN CHINA ALMOST 2,000 YEARS AGO.

Marge has made a list of things to pack for Bart's camping trip. But Bart has gone and scrambled all the letters. Can you figure out the ten items on Marge's list?

1. PINEBLAS EGG
2. CASPANKK
3. BOTTSHHURO
4. SPAMSOC
5. SPLAT APPERE
6. KNYSM SMUYAC
7. IDOAR
8. MES STARRAIT
9. WEEDURRAN
10. AMP

Now, see if you can take the first letters of each of the items and rearrange them to find out where Bart is going camping.

LISA'S IRRITATING DOT-AND-LINE INITIAL GAME

This is a game for two to four people. Fill a page with a grid of dots. The object of the game is to complete as many small boxes as possible. Take turns drawing a horizontal or vertical line between two of the dots. When a player closes up a box, he puts his initial inside the square and takes another turn. The person with the most initialed squares wins.

BACKYARD CARNIVAL

So. You're out on your butt, bored, and broke. What do you do? Well, in the words of one famous aging child star, "Hey! I've got an idea! Let's put on a show!" It's a time-honored tradition of raising money and entertaining yourself and others in the process. Just be careful not to spend more than you think you'll take in – –but don't charge so much you scare away customers! First, enlist and organize the neighborhood kids. Be sure to take full advantage of any unexpected help or talent someone may have to offer if they want to be included in your fun! Figure out who is going to do what: painting signs, collecting the materials you'll all need (does anyone have access to wood, paint, paper, old sheets, etc.?), building booths, making tickets, advertising, etc. Maybe you can find some parents to help finance the project! I know you hate to get them involved, but they do have resources and would probably be satisfied with ringside seats in return for their patronage. Who knows, they may even have some ideas of their own! So get out there and develop those all-important, entrepreneurial, management skills (coercion, creative finance, and discipline) that will be more useful to you later in life than you realize now. Make ribbons or bottle-cap medals as prizes and. . . on with the show!

THE LLAMA IS THE FIRST ANIMAL TO HAVE BEEN DOMESTICATED.

CAVALCADE OF CRITTERS

Get a few friends together to decorate all your bikes (we provide some ideas for this elsewhere in this book). Form a parade line (and maybe throw in a horn or whistle for extra attention), ride around your neighborhood and to adjoining blocks as a colorful advertisement of just how much fun your carnival will be. Dress up your pets and drag 'em along. Watch out for cars, man.

DOGMATIC CAT AND DOG TRICKS

If you've got willing pooches, set up a small obstacle course of easy jumps, or teach 'em how to shake hands or dance on two legs. Don't forget the dog's reward for a good performance – –a healthy bone or treat and lots of pats and hugs. You could also set up a short race course with a bowl of food at the end, and see who's the fastest (or hungriest) in the neighborhood. Good tricks to teach cats include sleeping, eating, yawning, and ignoring you on command.

CREEPY CRAWLY
BUG ZOO

THE WEIRDLY BEARDED LADY

Even if some lady you know actually has a beard, you'd better fake this one. There are a number of ways of doing this. For mere stubble or five-o'clock shadow, use the burnt end of a cork – – after it cools! – – to rub on the face. Otherwise, bits of an old wig or fake-fur material (usually found at fabric stores) could be used creatively to simulate a beard. Be sure to display her in a darkened setting – – backlighting gives a good, creepy effect.

PESKY PING-PONG FISHY PITCH

Get some cheap goldfish from your local pet store. Put them in large glasses filled with clean water and group the glasses closely together. Players stand back a few feet and toss ping-pong balls into the glasses. If the ball lands in the glass, the player wins the fish.

SQUISHY SQUIRT-GUN SHOOTOUT

This game is everything a good attraction should be. . . cheap, easy, and fun! Stack six or more paper cups on top of each other in a pyramid shape. Have people stand ten feet away and see how many cups they can knock down with five squirts from a water gun.

CREEPY CRAWLY BUG ZOO

This is a variant of the age-old flea circus scam where people would pay to see fleas perform tricks; when they got inside, they discovered that fleas were so small they couldn't see them! We suggest using bugs (which are visible) instead of fleas (unless you have incredible powers of persuasion!). You don't have to teach them actual tricks. Build different cages out of boxes, or decorate areas in one giant box, and have different bugs or lizards and things walking along ramps or going through tunnels or mini-mazes. A pet snake is always a good draw, especially when it's time to feed it!

USE PAPER INSTEAD OF PLASTIC WHEN SERVING FOOD AT YOUR FOOD BOOTH. EVERY TWO WEEKS, AMERICANS THROW AWAY ENOUGH GLASS BOTTLES AND CANS TO FILL UP THE WORLD TRADE CENTER TOWERS IN NEW YORK CITY.

INSTANT PHOTOGRAPHIC PERSONALITY TRANSPLANTS

Maybe you've seen these at real carnivals. You'll need access to an instant camera for this one. Using stiff cardboard, so they'll stand up, paint life-sized pictures of different people (real or imaginary), but cut a hole where the face should be. Have your customers stand behind the cut-outs with their faces stuck through the hole and take their picture!

SELL HOMEMADE LEMONADE!

What better way to spend a hot day than sitting around in the shade, achieving profits! Use the recipe below (if your mom or dad doesn't already have one) to make your own tasty lemonade. If there's no carnival, set up a stand in front of your own or a neighbor's house and sell it to all the hot, thirsty people that walk by. Make a big, eye-catching sign to tempt them. And don't drink all your supply!

Stir together until dissolved:
    6 Tablespoons SUGAR
    4 Cups WATER
Add :
    6 Tablespoons LEMON JUICE
Serve over crushed ice. To make pink lemonade, add a few drops of red food coloring.
Makes 4 servings.

MARGE'S BEEHIVE BEANBAG TOSS

Make your own beanbags out of the foot part of old socks – –fill them with sand and sew up the opening. You can also use old tennis balls. For a target, take a piece of wood or a large box and paint a picture of Marge on one side. Cut holes in her hair and mark different point values for each one. Contestants throw the beanbags or balls through the holes and add up their scores after three tries.

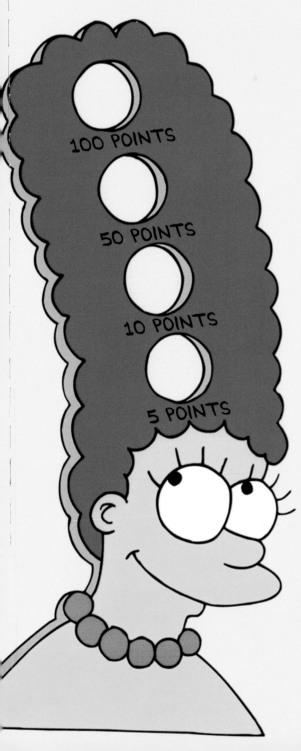

100 POINTS

50 POINTS

10 POINTS

5 POINTS

COUNT BARTULA'S INTERNATIONAL HOUSE OF SPOOKS

Find a room that you can make very dark, like the basement or garage. Set up a narrow passage that your victims must crawl along, between boxes and chairs and under tables. Drape sheets and blankets over the top. Along the path, hang spooky things like rubber spiders on strings and dangling moss, so people will brush against them. Make a silhouette of a scary scene, like a graveyard, with cardboard cutouts for tombstones and a branch for an old dead tree; set it up outside the passage, then briefly shine a flashlight on the scene so its shadow falls on the sheets. Lurk at an opening in the passage holding a flashlight under your chin. When victims approach, shine the light on your face for a second while making the most monstrous expression you can (try adding some ketchup "blood" to enhance the effect). Along the way, hand "body parts" to your victims: cold spaghetti for guts, a round, damp sponge for brains, and grapes or hardboiled eggs for eyes. Add further atmosphere with hideous screams, fiendish laughter, ghostly moaning, wolf howls, clanking chains, and creaking hinges!

Neighborhood OLYMPICS

Here's some fun you can have with a large, well-organized group of people. Doesn't sound like any group you know? Well, start one of these games and see how fast you can make 'em shape up! Figure out how many events you're going to have and make a gold, silver and bronze colored ribbon to give out as prizes for each event. Be sure to make multiple ribbons for the team events! Whoever has the most ribbons at the end of the day is the Neighborhood Olympic Champuion!

BACK-TO-BACK BALANCING ACT

Members of each team divide up into pairs. The first pair in each team stands back to back. At the signal, the third player in each team places a ball (or a water balloon) between the pair, who hold it in place with their backs. They must get to the turning line and return to the starting line holding the ball or balloon between them all the way, then passing it to the next pair on their team. If they drop it, they can pick it up and keep on going. Be sure to have a few extra water balloons handy!

PASS-THE-BUCK RELAY RACES

All relay games are fun, and we'll just give you a few choice examples to get you into the swing. Feel free to make up your own rules. All of them start with players split evenly into teams and lined up in columns by a starting line, about thirty feet from a turning line.

MADDENINGLY MUTANT THREE-LEGGED RACE

Members of each team divide up into pairs. Each pair of players ties their inside legs together at the ankle with a belt, piece of rope, or handkerchief. On the signal, each pair races forward toward the turning line and back again to the start. They tag the second pair, who do the same. The first team whose players all complete the race wins.

Fall-Flat-on-Your-Face Sack Race

The first player on each team holds a large cloth sack, the kind fifty pounds of potatoes come in. At a signal, he or she climbs into the sack, and, holding its open end up around their waist, jumps to the turning line and back, touches the next player and hands over the sack. The first team to have all players complete the action wins.

TOTALLY TENACIOUS TUG-O-WAR

This is how some of the borders of Eastern Europe were determined after World War I. We are just now seeing the effect this game can have on the world. To play it in your neighborhood, divide the players into two teams as evenly matched in strength and number as possible. The members of each team hold opposite ends of a rope about 25 feet long. Each team tries to pull the other over a line drawn halfway between them. If the line happens to run through a mud puddle, it adds an element of tension that is particularly thrilling. When a signal is given, the tug of war begins. The team which pulls the whole rope to its side of the line or puddle wins the game. Heave ho!

Devilishly Daring Egg Races

Here are two different games showing how much fun it can be to play with raw eggs! They are both relays involving a starting line and a turning line. In the first game, at the signal, players from each team start pushing eggs along the ground towards the turning line and back again...with their noses! The embarrassing term, "Egg on your face" may have come from the losers of this game!
In the second game, instead of pushing the egg along the ground, each player balances it on a spoon held in his or her mouth! This can be quite hazardous for the eggs, so be sure to have a few extras on hand.

PERILOUSLY PRECARIOUS HUMAN PYRAMIDS

See how many people you can stack up to form a human pyramid. Be sure to put the largest kids on the bottom row. This will form a sturdy base (the secret ingredient of all successful pyramids throughout history). Have the people on the bottom row line up shoulder to shoulder on their hands and knees. The next row climbs on top of them also on their hands and knees, straddling each member of the bottom row, like in a row of bricks. Each row will use one less person than the row underneath it. Stack as many rows as you can, with the smallest person in the group crowning the top of the whole pyramid. Be careful getting down!

Unbearable Wheelbarrow Races

Members of each team divide up into pairs. The first pair in each team assumes the wheelbarrow position: one player lies down on the ground with his palms on the ground; the second player lifts him by the ankles and makes him walk on his hands, guiding him like a wheelbarrow. At the starting signal, the first pair on each team races towards the turning line. At the turning line, they switch positions and race back to the starting line to touch the next pair, which has been waiting in wheelbarrow position. The first team to have all its players complete the action wins.

GROUP GAMES

SIMON SAYS

In this game, one person is chosen to be Simon and stands in front of the others who line up as indicated below. Simon has absolute power over the other players so be careful who you chose (or be sure to chose yourself). Simon makes the other players do all sorts of foolish things by saying, "Simon says...". Like "Simon says stand on your head." or "Simon says pat your head, rub your stomach and turn around in a circle on one leg while bleating like a sheep." See, power is fun! And absolute power is absolute fun! There is another wrinkle. If Simon doesn't say, "Simon says" before giving the instruction, and the players do it anyway, they are out of the game. The game is over when all the players are out, or they stage a coup, whichever comes first. Ideally, everyone would have a chance to be Simon. But its not an ideal world, now, is it?

MOTHER, MAY I?

This is absolute dictatorship in action, hence the name. One player, chosen to be "Mother," stands 20–30 feet in front of the others. Mother then tells each player in turn how many and what size steps they may take forward. For example, one giant step, two baby steps, three regular steps, etc. Before players can move, they must first ask, "Mother may I?" Mother must then say, "Yes, you may," or "No, you may not," before they proceed. Any player who takes steps without asking, "Mother, may I?" gets sent back to the start. The first player to tag Mother wins.

BASELINE

RED LIGHT, GREEN LIGHT

One player is chosen to be the "Lightkeeper," and stands 20–30 feet in front of the other players with his back towards them.

The "Lightkeeper" closes his eyes, says "Green Light," counts to 3, says "Red Light," turns around and opens his eyes. When the "Light-keeper" says "Green Light," the other players advance. When they hear "Red Light," they stop. If the "Lightkeeper" catches anyone moving when he turns around, the offender must go back to the baseline. Continue until someone gets close enough to tag the "Lightkeeper," who then turns around and chases the tagger to the base-line. If the "Lightkeeper" tags the runner, he remains the "Lightkeeper." If he doesn't, the runner becomes the new "Lightkeeper" and a new game begins.

SLAUGHTER BALL

You'll need a quiet street, empty parking lot, or a field, about 10 kids, one ball like a basketball or volleyball, and a lot of aggression to play this game, a variation of Dodge Ball. Split into teams A and B. Put one person in the "OUT" box for each team and the rest in the "IN" boxes. Team A gets the ball first, throwing it back and forth between their "IN" and "OUT" boxes. They throw the ball at the players in the Team B "IN" box, who try to dodge it. If a player gets hit, that player must go to their "OUT" box. However, if the ball is thrown at a player and they catch it, they are safe. The object is to eliminate all the other team members from their "IN" box. The first team to do so wins the game. Sounds like fun, huh! It is. Until you get smacked in the head by the ball! Duck, you idiot!

TEAM B "OUT" BOX

TEAM A "IN" BOX

TEAM B "IN" BOX

TEAM A "OUT" BOX

RED ROVER

This is a great outdoor game that should appeal to every taste. Even Marge likes this game because its not too violent, while at the same time being very active and fun. Two teams line up at their respective baselines about 30 feet apart. They each form a chain by linking elbows with the people on either side of them. The player at one end of line A starts by calling out "Red Rover, Red Rover, send (name of person on Team B) right over!" That person breaks out of Team B's line, runs towards Team A's line and tries to break through between any two people. If they are successful, they get to chose the player of their choice from Team A and bring them back to join Team B. If they are unsuccessful at breaking through Team A's line, then they must join Team A. Then it's Team B's turn to yell "Red Rover..." and try to have someone break through their line. Take turns up and down the line yelling "Red Rover...". The game ends when one team is down to its last player and can't form a chain

BUM, BUM, BUM, HERE WE COME

This great game combines action and imagination, a potent combination! It's known in different versions throughout the country but here is the version the Simpsons play. Split into two teams like in Red Rover, only don't join arms. Team A huddles up and decides on something that they are going to imitate by acting out. Once they decide what they're going to be (a windmill, robots, airplanes, tigers, etc.), they form back into their line and start the call. This is the call:

Team A: "Bum, bum, bum, here we come,
　　　　　All the way from Washington!"
Team B: "What's your trade?"
Team A: "Sweet lemonade!"
Team B: "Then hurry up and get it made!"

As this call and response is taking place, Team A moves down the field towards Team B's baseline. They stop just short of Team B and start acting out whatever it is they have chosen to be in pantomime. Team B starts trying to guess what Team A is acting out. As soon as someone on Team B guesses correctly, Team A shouts out confirmation and starts running back towards their own baseline. Once they cross their baseline, they're safe. Team B chases them trying to tag as many players as possible. Whoever they tag then joins Team B and it then becomes Team B's turn to think of something to be. The game ends when there are no players left on one team.

TEAM A

○ ○ ○ ○ ○ ○ ○

> REMEMBER, MAN, IT'S NOT WHETHER YOU WIN OR LOSE, IT'S WHO YOU CHOOSE TO BRUISE!

X X X X X X X

TEAM B

THE AVERAGE LIFE EXPECTANCY OF A PROFESSIONAL FOOTBALL PLAYER IS 56 YEARS.

COACH

Crocodiles cannot chew. Neither can a worm.

The sperm whale has the world's largest teeth – ten inches long.

A Day at the Beach

BODY SCULPTING

Try your hand at cosmetic sand surgery – cover as much of a friend as you want with a solid layer of sand (leave their heads and arms free to give orders, of course), then let your imagination go to work. Wetter sand makes better body parts. If you've semi-buried your mother, you'll also find this is a good time to finish off those cookies she wouldn't let you have any more of...

BURIED TREASURE HUNT

Bury a treasure chest in the sand and then create your own treasure map to guide your friends to the site. Before burying, wrap the treasure in a plastic bag, then put it in a cardboard box covered with tinfoil so the sand doesn't get inside.
Then draw an elaborate map, using landmarks along the shoreline ("Take three steps from the driftwood log towards the condo, then six jumps towards the barbecue pit"). Use more mysterious word clues for more challenge ("When the sun is at its peak, follow the shadow from the taller pole holding up the volleyball net seven steps," etc.)

Water Balloon Toss

Play this game in teams of two. Pairs stand opposite each other, forming two lines. One partner holds a full water balloon and tosses it to his teammate. With each toss, the partners step further and further back from each other. The last pair remaining high and dry wins.

Beachside Real Estate Development

Use slightly wet sand for strong foundations. Make towers, parapets, and various spooky nooks and crannies by taking a handful of sand that's been soaking in the bottom of a bucket of water and squeezing it carefully through your fist into a tall heap (it will look like candle drippings). Add tunnels and moats, drawbridges made of seashells and driftwood, and beachglass windows. Make sure your site is above the high-tide line, or you'll be all washed up before you know it!

If you break open a dried sand dollar carefully, you'll find five tiny white pieces shaped like doves inside.

Sharks burp to regulate their depth underwater

UNDERWATER SPY CAMERA

Secrets of the Deep Revealed!

Scope out what's going on down under with this instant underwater viewer. Cut the top and bottom off an empty coffee can or half-gallon milk carton. Stretch a sheet of clear plastic kitchen wrap tightly over the bottom. Hold it in place securely with a couple of tight rubber bands (or lots of Scotch tape). Don't lower it too far into the water or you might spring an untimely leak.

Beachside Beauty Tips

Seashells make excellent necklaces (look for periwinkles or small scallop shells that already have little holes for stringing), earrings or barrettes (glue them onto plain plastic clips), or bracelets (loop them on an elastic band or piece of string). If the shells are a little smelly from the water, leave them overnight in a bucket full of fresh water and a cup of liquid bleach.

Remember to use plenty of suntan lotion whenever you're out — even when it's cloudy — unless you want to turn into a human sundried tomato!

SANDWICH-O-MATIC

Peanut butter	Sliced bananas	Mayonnaise
Cream cheese	Chopped nuts	Honey
Sliced cheese	Sliced cucumber	Maple syrup
Ham	Lettuce	Mustard
Chicken	Chopped celery	Jelly
Tuna fish	Chopped carrots	Sunflower seeds
Liverwurst	Bean sprouts	Raisins
Turkey	Tomato slices	Sesame seeds
Cottage cheese	Apple slices	Fresh parsley
Bacon strips	Chopped pickles	Jam
	Slice of onion	

Choose one (or more) items from each column, and assemble between slices of bread for a monster gourmet treat.

The seahorse swims at the rate of one foot per minute.

The internal organs of the antarctic sea spider are in its legs.

HELP! TRAPPED DESERT ISLAND! GUY WITH A BANJO

BEACHBALL BOOGIE

Teams of two race to a finish line, balancing an inflated beachball between their noses. Don't drop the ball, or you'll be outta the race...

Jellyfish have no blood.

The electric eel can discharge one hundred watts of electricity from 30 to 300 times a minute.

Frogs have teeth; toads don't.

THE WONDERFUL WORLD OF WACKY WAXED PAPER STAINED-GLASS PRESSINGS

These pressings make great fake stained-glass windows. They can also make wonderful seasonal placemats. Autumn leaves are best because they're so brightly colored, and pressing them makes the colors last. Press flowers for a springtime effect.

First dry the flowers and leaves you've collected. Put them between two sheets of clean paper & place them inside a big, thick book. They should be dry in a couple of weeks. Then cut two pieces of waxed paper the same size. Arrange dried leaves or flowers on one sheet, waxed side up. Add bits of shaved crayons and glitter. Put the other sheet on top (waxed side down) and place these between several sheets of newspaper. Press very quickly with a warm iron. Let it cool before using it.

COOL, MAN!

BART'S PIRATE POTATO PRINTS

This is what Gutenberg spent his childhood doing. As an adult, he grew dissatisfied with the texture of a potato. For our purposes, though, it's perfect. Cut a large potato in half and blot moisture from it with a paper towel. Draw a simple design on the cut part with a felt-tipped marker. Cut around your design with a knife, leaving the design raised above the potato's surface. Pour a little poster paint into a plate and either dip your potato in it or spread it lightly over the cut surface with a paintbrush. Press the painted potato onto a piece of paper and lift carefully to see your print. It's a great way to make cards or, if you repeat the print in a pattern, cool wrapping paper, man.

THIS IS YOUR LIFE

Nature is pretty weird, man. When people call something a freak of nature, it's about as freaky as a thing can get. This shouldn't always be scary. Sometimes you can just sit back and enjoy it. You can even be inspired by it! Imagine a giant albino whale or a monster tornado. Pretty strange things by themselves, but Melville wrote "Moby Dick" and we've all seen the "Wizard of Oz." See the way totally weird things can be turned into something cool? So keep a journal of whatever strange stuff happens to you. Then you can use it as a starting point to make up your own stories that no one will believe.

And Picasso probably never saw a three-eyed woman, but you wouldn't know it by looking at some of his drawings! So don't be inhibited by reality. Create your own reality. Remember, to an empty page, you are God.

JUNGLE JOURNAL JUICE

Collect a bunch of ripe cherries, blueberries, strawberries, or blackberries. Take off the stems and leaves. Crush the berries in a small cup. Add a little water and stir well. Put a paper towel over a small jar, pushing it down into the jar. Pour the berry juice onto the paper towel until it all drains through. Remove the paper towel. Use a fountain pen or a sharp stick to write with. Be sure to put the lid on the jar when you're through.

A CHIP OFF THE OLD ROCK

The cave paintings in Lascaux, France, are over 15,000 years old! The cavepeople who painted them made their own paints from crushed rocks and minerals mixed with water, blood, or animal fat for binding. Today we have other options for binders, but we can still make our own paint. Use red clay for red, charcoal for black, white clay or lime for white, and ocher for yellows. Crush your minerals with a hammer or a mortar and pestle, and mix them with liquid starch, soap flakes and water, corn starch, corn syrup, or egg yolks to bind them into paint. Check out the labels of storebought paints to get ideas for other minerals to use for other colors

IN SHAKESPEARE'S OWN TIME HIS NAME WAS SPELLED IN 83 DIFFERENT WAYS.

catch THE Wind

GUSTY GIMMICKS

WIND CHIMES are great things to make and have around, especially if you have cats — they'll drive 'em crazy! So be sure to put them up high. They can be made out of just about anything. Shells are great, wood is nice if it's hollow like bamboo, or try bits of glass, metal, or anything that makes a pleasing sound when it's struck. Even old silverware or tin can lids can be painted and turned into twirling art.

MOBILES don't make noise. Use anything light or flat that will catch the wind and look interesting as it twirls, like feathers, shells, bark, etc. Collect small branches and hang your objects from them with fishing line or thread. See how large you can make one by using a big branch at the top, and hanging smaller, thinner branches from that.

TEMPESTUOUS TRASHBAG KITE

(TOP OF BAG)

29" 10" 6.5" 5" 6" 12"

This kite is as easy to fly as it is to make. Lay a plastic 13-gallon (kitchen size) garbage bag flat. Measure the cutting lines as shown in the diagram, and mark them with a felt-tip pen. Cut along the lines, cutting away the shaded areas.

Open up the bag. Decorate or draw a design or funny face on the surface of the bag. Let it dry. Turn the kite over and tape the dowels or straight sticks in position. Use six pieces of tape for each dowel, as shown. Reinforce the corners of the cutout area and the wing tips with extra tape. Poke a tiny hole in each wing tip. Cut a piece of string ten feet long. Tie each end through the holes in the wing tips. This is the kite's bridle. Tie a loop at the end of the bridle. Attach the flying line to the loop. Take it outside for a test flight to see if it needs a tail. Use some thick string, yarn, or bits of cloth or newspaper to make one.

MAKE A MULTI-COLORED
PINWHEEL

This'll set your mind awhirl! Cut the diagram below along the dotted lines. Bend the corners in to the center in sequential order. Stick a pin through all the corners and the center of the pinwheel, sticking it to a straw or the eraser on the tip of a long pencil. Hold it with the pinned side toward the wind and watch it twirl!

1

2

4

3

GALACTIC GOLF

HOLE #3

HOLE #4

HOLE #7

HOLE #9

HOLE #6

HOLE #5

WEATHER HAS SIX MAIN COMPONENTS: TEMPERATURE, ATMOSPHERIC PRESSURE, WIND, HUMIDITY, PRECIPITATION AND TV WEATHERMEN.

HOLE #2

HOLE #8

Find a large open area like a park, a playground, or an unused school campus. You could even use your whole neighborhood. Pick out large, visible objects (trees, street lamps, flagpoles, even fire hydrants, etc.) to use as "holes." The farther from each other they are, the better. Assign a number to each "hole" to set up the course. Standing at the starting point, throw your frisbee at the first hole. If you hit it, it's a "hole in one." If you miss, pick up the frisbee wherever it lands, and try again until you make it. Then, from that hole, aim at the next one. Any number of players may play, but each player must hit every hole in sequence. The player using the least number of throws (strokes) to complete the course wins.

HOLE #1

IMPROVE YOUR GAME!

WITH THIS CLAY POT WIND VANE

Insert a pencil into the drainage hole of an upside-down flower pot, eraser end up. Secure it with some clay or chewing gum. Make two triangles of stiff paper. Cut slits in the ends of a straw and glue the triangles into them. Attach the straw to the pencil eraser with a pin, making sure it moves freely. It will point in the direction the wind is coming from. Now you don't need a weatherman to know which way the wind blows!

W   S

Lisa "Earhart" Simpson's Anti-Air-Bart
GLIDER

Take to the skies with this aerodynamically accurate lighter-than-air cruiser. Watch out for crash landings, though, unless you want to follow Amelia Earhart into the mysterious mist!

1. Fold along central line and make a small pinch halfway down.

2. Fold bottom edge up to center point.

3. Fold each corner of the bottom in towards edge.

4. Diagonally fold each side of bottom towards center fold.

5. Tuck the tip under and behind, to meet the center point.

6. Fold in half vertically.

7. Fold each of the already-folded edges back (outwards) toward center fold.

8. Open wings out to form right angles. Curl the trailing ends by pulling them across the edge of a table or around a pencil.

A CLOUD AT GROUND LEVEL IS CALLED MIST IF VISIBILITY IS GREATER THAN ONE KILOMETER. IF VISIBILITY IS LESS THAN ONE KILOMETER, IT IS CALLED FOG.

9. Soar away!

Follow the instructions on the previous page to create your very own Anti-Air-Bart glider. Of course, you don't have to limit yourself to Bart--use your aircraft to attack anyone you please...or just fly it for fun! By cutting out the square below, you will have quite a sturdy airplane that should survive many missions. Happy landings!

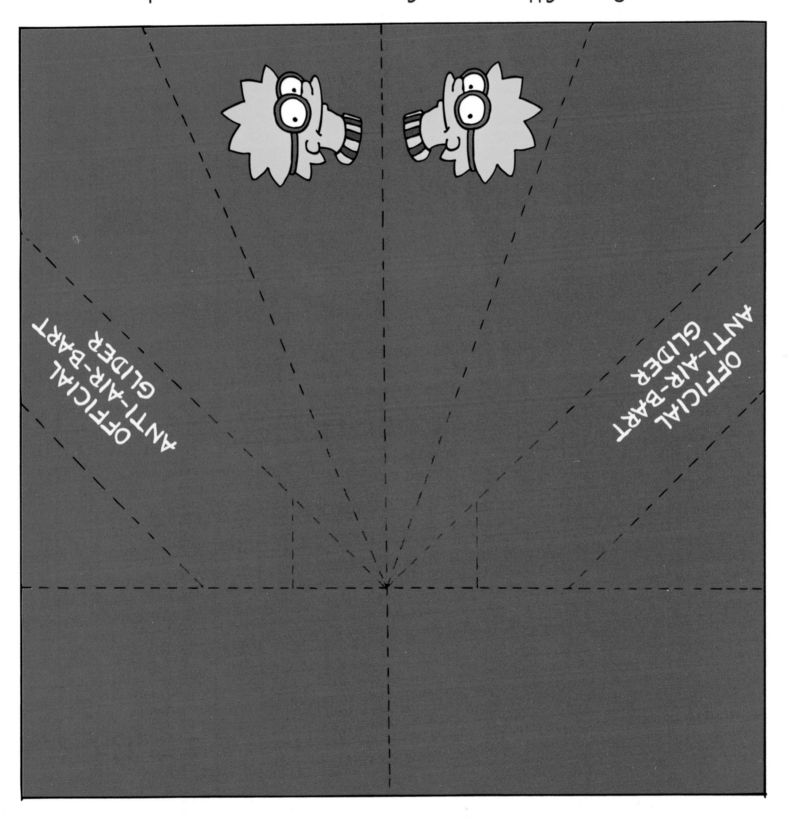

CUT-OUT ALONG SOLID LINE, FOLD ALONG DOTTED LINES

These are the **PINK SLIPS** and **INDEX CARDS** for "THE PARTY AT THE BURNS MANSION," a game in this book. Cut 'em out and stack 'em face down to play the game.

INDEX CARD	INDEX CARD	INDEX CARD	PINK SLIP	PINK SLIP	PINK SLIP
INDEX CARD	INDEX CARD	INDEX CARD	PINK SLIP	PINK SLIP	PINK SLIP
INDEX CARD	INDEX CARD	INDEX CARD	PINK SLIP	PINK SLIP	PINK SLIP
INDEX CARD	INDEX CARD	INDEX CARD	PINK SLIP	PINK SLIP	PINK SLIP
INDEX CARD	INDEX CARD	INDEX CARD	PINK SLIP	PINK SLIP	PINK SLIP

THE ANSWERS!!

ANSWERS TO "MARGE'S MIXED-UP JUMBLE":

1. SLEEPING BAG
2. KNAPSACK
3. TOOTHBRUSH
4. COMPASS
5. PAPER PLATES
6. YUMMY SNACKS
7. RADIO
8. AIR MATTRESS
9. UNDERWEAR
10. MAP

He's going to CAMP KRUSTY

"SAY WHAT?" DOUBLE ACROSTIC SOLUTION:

MARGE
"I REALLY LOVE MY BIG HAIRDO."

A. Moby
B. Airhead
C. R.I.
D. Golly
E. Evil

THE SOLUTION TO "THE CASE OF THE MISSING CASE":

Someone in the tavern grabbed the case of Duff beer and put it up on top of the TV. Homer couldn't have done it because he was sitting right in front of the phone watching the Monster Truck Rally on TV. Besides, Moe would have seen him. Sam had his right arm in a cast, so he couldn't have managed to lift the case so quickly and quietly. Larry was certainly in a good position to nab the case. However, Larry's hands are covered with bright blue pool cue chalk, and there was no blue chalk found on the case of Duff. Ned Flanders was jogging past the tavern, but he would never patronize a dive like Moe's, let alone steal a case of Duff beer from there! He doesn't even like Duff! It's very unlikely Police Chief Wiggum would have taken it, and so that leaves the guy at the end of the bar. He could have easily grabbed the case and then, seeing the police chief about to come in, shoved it up on top of the TV and gone back to reading his sleazy tabloid... but not before getting his ink-stained fingerprints all over the case!

If you recognized this mystery man as Moe's best customer, Barney, you know this case of the missing case was just a practical joke on Moe!

THE HIDDEN ITEMS IN "WHITE WATER WIPEOUT":

A rose
A spoon
A bowl
A phone
A peeled banana
A catcher's mitt
A submarine sandwich
Headphones
A bullhorn
A thermos
A trombone
A candle
A roasted turkey
A screwdriver
A stalk of celery
A sailor's hat
A rope
An apple
A fishing pole
A trashcan lid
A glass of beer
A rifle
A fire extinguisher
A butcher's knife

PICNIC PANIC!

HOT DOG
SLINGSHOT
BABY BOTTLE
PORK CHOP
FISH
PENCIL
RATTLE
SWIM FIN
CUPCAKE
SODA CAN
SAXOPHONE
CLOCK
SPRAY CAN
SLICE OF PIZZA
BOWLING BALL
FOOTBALL
BASEBALL
GOLF CLUB
LUNCH PAIL
FRIED EGG
DONUT
ICE CREAM CONE
GELATIN DESSERT

OH, MAN!

WHO SWIPED THE CUPCAKES?

ANSWER:
Maggie wanted the cupcakes, but couldn't reach them. Lisa was much too intent on her studies to even notice them. Bart looks guilty, but Bart always looks guilty. Snowball II looks suspicious enough, but since Marge's yummy cupcakes contain NO tuna or tuna by-products, she lacks motivation. Homer had the opportunity, the means and, knowing the cupcakes were intended for Patty and Selma, the motivation. It was Homer, all right. He stashed the cupcakes behind the toaster just as Marge left the kitchen and quickly turned his back on everyone else in the room.

MARGE'S WEEK-AT-A-GLANCE:
E, C, B, F, A, D

UH OH!

I'M BART SIMPSON WHO THE HELL ARE YOU

DOUBLE ACROSTIC: ANSWER EACH OF THE QUESTIONS BELOW. THEN ENTER THE LETTERS INTO THE BOXES ABOVE ACCORDING TO THE NUMBERS INDICATED.

A. Word before dog or foot or rod. HOT

B. Weak; spineless. WIMPY

C. Head of the House of Simpson. HOMER

D. What Bart is to the above. SON

E. John or Paul or George or Ringo. BEATLE

F. Ben's last name. HUR

G. Simpson sibling. LISA

Otto's WILD RIDE!

DEAD END
TOXIC SPILL
FALLEN TREE
ROAD FLOODED
WORLD'S LARGEST POTHOLE
MEN AT WORK
GARAGE SALE
BRIDGE OUT

REVEALED AT LAST!
SOLUTIONS
TO OUR BAFFLING PUZZLES!

NO PEEKING, YOU TWO!

ANSWER: Lisa goes through the maze, but Bart cheats and gets there first.

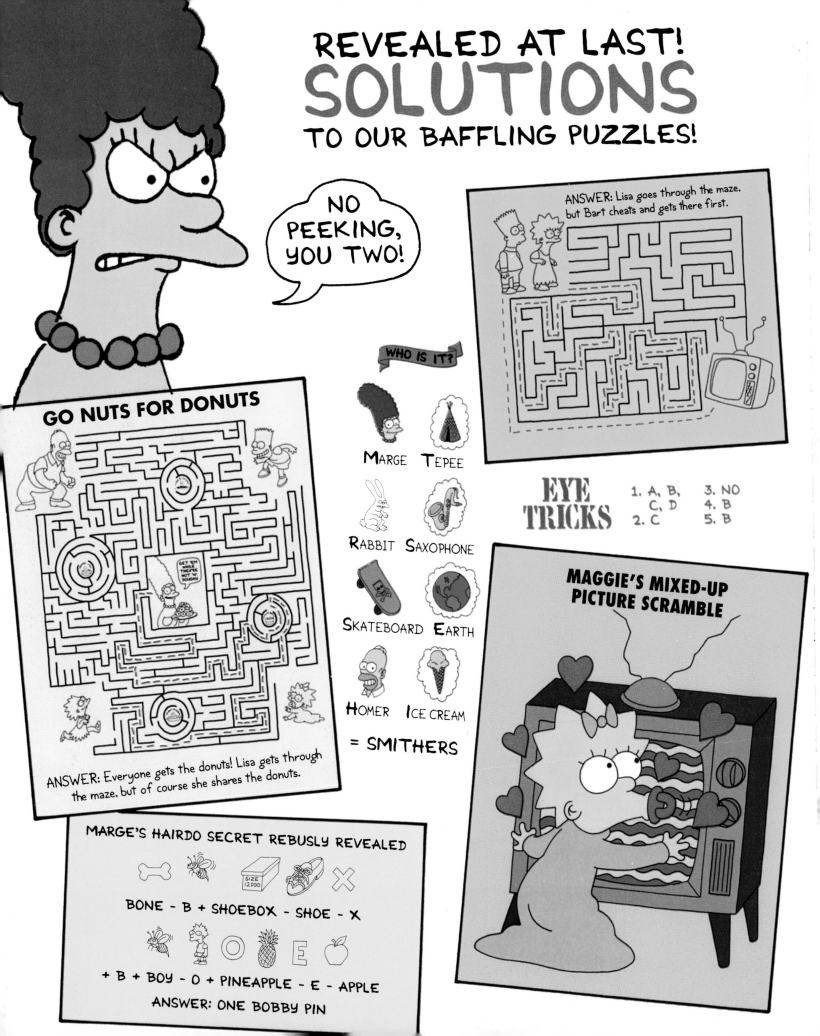

GO NUTS FOR DONUTS

GET 'EM WHILE THEY'RE HOT 'N' DOUGHY!

ANSWER: Everyone gets the donuts! Lisa gets through the maze, but of course she shares the donuts.

WHO IS IT?

MARGE   TEPEE

RABBIT   SAXOPHONE

SKATEBOARD   EARTH

HOMER   ICE CREAM

= SMITHERS

EYE TRICKS

1. A, B, C, D
2. C
3. NO
4. B
5. B

MAGGIE'S MIXED-UP PICTURE SCRAMBLE

MARGE'S HAIRDO SECRET REBUSLY REVEALED

BONE - B + SHOEBOX - SHOE - X

+ B + BOY - O + PINEAPPLE - E - APPLE

ANSWER: ONE BOBBY PIN

THE SIMPSONS'
HECK-OF-A-LOT MORE
CARD GAMES

PIG

For 3 to 13 players. Select as many four-of-a-kinds as there are players (for example, if you have four players, you'll use sixteen cards -- say, four Homers, four Marges, four Lisas and four fours). Shuffle and deal them out. Each player looks at his or her hand and then passes a card to the player on the left, and then another and another, the faster the better. As soon as anyone gets four-of-a-kind, he or she puts his or her finger on his nose and stops passing. As soon as you see someone do so, put your finger on your nose. The last one to do so loses. Appropriate pig sounds may be made at this (or any other) point in the game.

PYRAMID

Lay 28 cards out in a pyramid, starting with one at the top, overlapping two beneath that, etc. The bottom row should have 7 cards. You remove any pair in the bottom row whose face value adds up to 13 and then any other such pair exposed as cards are removed (Jacks=11, Queens=12, Kings=13, Aces=1). The undealt cards are turned over one at a time, and can be used with whatever cards on the board are completely exposed. If you tear down the whole pyramid, you win.

RAIDING THE REFRIGERATOR

For 2 to 4 players. Deal everyone four cards, and place four cards face-up in the center--those are the midnight snacks. The rest of the cards are left face-down in one pile in the center, the pantry. You can steal food out of the fridge only if you have the matching card in your hand. Players go around in a circle, claiming their snacks by showing the card of the same rank from their hand, and placing their booty face-up in front of them. But watch out! If someone else has the same card too, he or she can swipe it from under your nose when it's his or her turn (you can't gorge yourself until the game is over). If it's your turn and you can't either raid the fridge or swipe a snack from someone else, you have to place one of your own cards face-up in the center. When everyone's hands (and stomachs) are empty, deal out four new helpings. Whoever ends up with his or her plate piled the highest wins.

INDIAN HEAD POKER

Deal one card face-down to each player. At the count of three, everyone holds the card up to his or her forehead facing out. Starting with the player to the left of the dealer, bet on whether you think your card is the high card of the bunch. When the bets are all in put the cards on the table. High card wins.

52 PICK-UP

Throw the deck into the air (preferably in a room where there's a huge amount of junk lying around already) and announce that the person who picks up the most cards wins. Then leave the room and head for the cookie jar before anyone notices you're gone. This game works only once per lifetime.

THE SIMPSONS' HECK-OF-A-DECK OF CARD GAMES

OLD MAIDS

For 3 to 5 players. The object of this game is to get rid of all your cards and NOT to get stuck with the "OLD MAIDS" card. Deal out all the cards, using only one of the two "OLD MAIDS" cards. Everyone sets down any pairs in his or her hand face up on the table. The player on the dealer's left holds out his or her cards face-down to the player on his or her left, who picks a card. Then that player does the same to the next player. Anytime you get a pair, set it down on the table. When you're out of cards (all have been paired off), you're safely out of the game. Sooner or later, everyone will drop out except the one holding the "OLD MAIDS."

CONCENTRATION

Deal all the cards out on a table, face down, in rows or in any pattern you'd like. Players take turns at turning two cards at a time face up. Whenever they make a matching pair, you keep them in your pile. If they don't match, you turn them face down again, and the next player tries. The winner is the person with the most cards when all of them have been removed from the table.

WAR

For 2 players. Deal out the whole deck face down in a pile in front of each player. Both players turn their top cards over at the same time. The one with the high card takes both and puts them under his stack. (In this game the ace is low and the king is high.) If the cards are the same value, "War" is declared. Each player turns up another card; the high card takes all four cards. If there's another tie, do it again until someone gets the high card. The winner is the one holding all the cards at the end.

SLAPBART

Use all the Bart/Joker cards. Deal all the cards out to the players, in face-down stacks. Everyone takes a turn turning over his or her top card into a center pile. When a Bart/Joker turns up, the first person to slap it with his or her hand wins all the cards in the center stack.

BLENDERIZED DELECTABLE GUZZLERS

Whiz around for about 15 seconds:

A Cup of yogurt + a Cup of any fruit juice + a handful of ice cubes

Half a banana (in chunks) + a Cup of orange juice + a dash of ginger

A Cup of yogurt + a Cup of fruit, fresh or frozen or even canned. Add a little cinnamon for spice.

A Cup of milk + a Tablespoon each of cocoa powder and of sugar or honey + a dash each of vanilla extract and cinnamon + a handful of ice cubes

A Scoop of ice cream + 1/2 Cup milk + a half banana, chunked + two dashes of cocoa powder and some cinnamon

HAND-MASHED SANDWICH SPREADS

Mash by hand:
1/2 Cup peanut butter + 1 large banana and a dash of cinnamon and/or coconut + a fingerful of raisins

OR

1/2 Cup peanut butter + 1/2 Cup softened cream cheese + a little honey + a few raisins

SUGARY SUGAR COOKIES

Turn on oven and make sure you have the following yum-licious ingredients:

400°

3/4 Cup butter or margarine. Use butter for a buttery taste. Use margarine for a sort of buttery taste.

1 Teaspoon vanilla... the extracted kind.

1 Cup pure white fallen sugar granules.

3/4 Cup of all-purpose flour after major nutrients have been taken out and put back in again.

2 eggs from either ranch-fed or chemically injected chickens. There's no taste difference anyway.

1 Teaspoon each baking powder and salt. (Use salt substitute if you're worried.)

☆ (☆ ☆ OKAY, WE CAN BEGIN ☆ (☆

In a large bowl of an electric mixer, beat butter and sugar until creamy, then beat in eggs and vanilla. In another bowl, stir together flour, baking powder and salt; gradually add this to butter mixture, blending thoroughly, to form a soft dough. Cover tightly with plastic wrap and refrigerate until firm (at least 1 hour or for up to 3 days).

On a floured board, roll out dough, a portion at a time, to a thickness of 1/8 inch (keep remaining portions refrigerated). Cut out with cookie cutters (about 2 1/2 inches in diameter) and place slightly apart on ungreased baking sheets. Sprinkle generously with sugar.

Bake at 400° in the oven for 8 to 10 minutes or until edges are lightly browned. Transfer to racks and let cool completely before handling. Store airtight in a hiding place that kids don't know about. Makes about 4 dozen scrump-tastic cookies. Should last a few days in a normal household. At our house, they're gone in 20 minutes.

OPTIONAL — For Marge's extra special "MULTICOLORED" cookies, just add a few drops of food coloring to each portion.

YOUR STOMACH IS THE SIZE OF A GRAPEFRUIT.

SOME-MORES
(Atomic Style)

Break off a piece of a chocolate bar and place it on a graham cracker and then put a marshmallow on top. Pop into the microwave, nuke 'em for a few seconds. Voila!

MESSIN' UP THE KITCHEN!

ICKY STICKS

(Not that kind. The kind you eat!)

Boil rapidly 2 cups of sugar, 2/3 cup of white corn syrup and 1/2 cup of water. It's done when you drop a small amount of the goop into a glass of cold water and it turns brittle. Remove from the range and stir in your favorite flavoring extract and food coloring. Drop by tablespoonfuls onto a greased cookie sheet and press a plastic spoon or fork into each one. They'll harden on the counter for consumption in an hour or so.

SCRUMPTIOUS SNAPPY POPCORN TOPPERS

Melt a little butter or margarine together with one of the following, and toss it into your next batch of freshly microwaved popcorn:

1/4 Teaspoon garlic powder (STINKY corn)
1/4 Cup shredded cheese (SLIMY corn)
1 Tablespoon peanut butter (STICKY corn)
2 Tablespoons brown sugar and
   a dash of cinnamon (SWEETY corn)
1/2 Teaspoon curry powder (SASSY corn)
1/2 Teaspoon chili powder (SPICY corn)

COWS HAVE FOUR STOMACHS.

IF YOU HOLD YOUR NOSE WHILE YOU EAT, YOU WON'T TASTE YOUR FOOD.

MAGGIE'S MUDPIES

One Cup dirt
1/2 Cup water
Tasty additions: small pebbles, dried leaves, bugs, plastic toys, worms.

Mix thoroughly. Shape into pies (or cupcakes). Bake on a hot sidewalk for 15 minutes. Eat. Or wear!

BART'S DOG-URRITOS

Boil one hotdog. Open one can of chili and heat it up in a pan. Grate up a little American cheese (or processed cheese food, for that ol' fashioned additive flavor). Wrap the dog, some chili and the cheese in a flour tortilla. Presto!

INSTANT PEANUT BUTTER BALLS

Mash together in a large bowl: 1 cup crunchy peanut butter and 1/2 cup dry milk powder and 1 cup shredded coconut and 1 teaspoon vanilla extract and 1 cup chopped dates or raisins. Roll the delectable mess into bite-sized balls, coat with sesame seeds and pop into your mouth. If you can manage not to eat them all, store the leftovers in the fridge.

Loop -the- Loop Airplane

1.

2.

3.

4.

Start with an 8 1/2" square of paper. Fold it in half diagonally. Open and make the two side folds (Fig. 1). Fold tip down about 1 1/2" past point A (Fig. 2). Next fold the tip upward so it extends about 1" above the body (Fig. 3). Now fold the tip down 1/2" as shown by the dotted line in Fig. 3. Turn the paper over. Make the two sides fold toward the middle (Fig. 4). These are the wings. Turn over again and fold it in half along the middle crease. Pick up the glider and turn up the wings so they stand out at right angles to the body. Squeeze the middle fold between your thumb and forefinger. Throw it STRAIGHT UP with the folded tip in front. It will come right back to you! If you throw it like a regular paper airplane it will fly toward the ground.

Gyrating GYROCOPTER

You can either use this one or copy it onto another piece of paper. Cut out along the heavy black lines. Don't cut along the dotted lines. Fold on lines A and B. Staple the sides together or wind some tape around them to keep them together. Now fold the blades along line C, bending one blade in one direction and the other blade in the opposite direction. Stand on some high place, hold by the bottom with the blades spread out and let go!

THE BIG POPPER

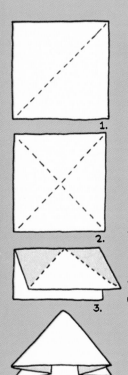

1.

2.

3.

4.

Take a big square sheet of newspaper. Fold diagonally corner to corner (Fig. 1). Open and fold the other corners the same way (Fig. 2). Open up and then fold in half (Fig. 3). Push in the shaded areas, making the folds sharp (Fig. 4). Hold with your pointer finger in between two of the points (Fig. 5) and snap your wrist down hard. The fold on the other side will snap out with a loud pop! Just tuck it back in to use again and again.

5.

PAPER-MANIA

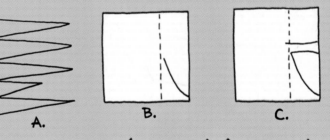

> WHOA, MAMA!!!

> LOOKS LIKE THAT ONE GOT TOO CLOSE TO THE NUCLEAR POWER PLANT!

Teenage Mutant PAPERDOLLS

You'll need a strip of paper 2" to 4" wide and 24" to 27" long. You can make it by cutting several sheets of paper lengthwise and sticking them together with clear tape. Fold the strip into eight or nine 3" accordion folds, but have one of the folds go only about half way, as in Fig. A. Make this fold the second or third fold. The dotted lines in Figs. B, C and D indicate the edge of the half fold. Make the first cut (No. 1), almost to this edge. Follow Fig. C and D to finish the cutout. It will look like Fig. E when it's unfolded.

A.

B.

C.

D.

E.

THE BAFFLING MOBIUS STRIP

CUT OUT A STRIP OF PAPER AT LEAST 12 INCHES LONG AND ABOUT 2 INCHES WIDE. MAKE ONE TWIST IN IT, THEN TAPE THE TWO ENDS TOGETHER. TRY TO FIGURE OUT WHICH SIDE IS WHICH BY DRAWING A SINGLE LINE LENGTHWISE DOWN ONE SIDE. HAVING A LITTLE TROUBLE? NOW CUT ALONG THAT LINE, ALL THE WAY AROUND THE LENGTH OF THE STRIP. YOU THINK YOU'LL GET TWO CIRCLES NOW, RIGHT? HA! TRY IT AND SEE!

Spinning Spiral Thingy

CUT OUT OR COPY THE SPIRAL. BE CAREFUL TO FOLLOW THE LINES. MAKE A SMALL DENT IN THE PAPER WHERE THE DOT IS SO IT WON'T SLIP OFF THE POINT, THEN BALANCE IT ON A PENCIL AS SHOWN. NOW HOLD IT OVER A LIGHTED ELECTRIC BULB AND WATCH IT SPIN!

DENT

Silly Shady SILHOUETTES

YOU CAN ALSO USE THE LAMP TO DRAW A SILHOUETTE. TAPE A PIECE OF PAPER TO THE WALL WHERE THE SHADOWS ARE CAST. NOW, HAVE YOUR FRIEND POSITION HERSELF SO THAT HER PROFILE CASTS A SHADOW ON THE PAPER. BY TRACING AROUND HER SHADOW, YOU DRAW A SILHOUETTE.

Lights Out! It's Time for
HANDY SHADOW SHOWS

TURN OFF ALL THE LIGHTS EXCEPT ONE LAMP. POSITION THE LAMP SO THAT IT SHINES ON A BLANK WALL. YOUR HANDS SHOULD BE ABOUT 3 FEET FROM THE LIGHT AND ABOUT 4 FEET FROM THE WALL. THE NEARER YOUR HANDS ARE TO THE LIGHT, THE LARGER AND LESS DISTINCT THE SHADOW WILL BE ON THE WALL. NOW, ARRANGE YOUR HANDS AND FINGERS IN THE POSITIONS SHOWN TO MAKE THESE FIGURES.

Like This!

RABBIT   LAMP

RAMPAGING ELEPHANT

VICIOUS WOLF

PECULIAR PIG

CACKLING GOOSE

RABID BEAR

FUNKY REGGAE SINGER

BART

ANNOYING ROOSTER

PESKY GOAT

TRY TO CREATE OTHER SHADOW PICTURES!

Sideshow Bob's
FLIPPED OUT
FLIP BOOK

> GO AHEAD AND FLIP IT. SEE IF I CARE.

Carefully cut along the heavy black lines on the next page. Try to keep the lines very straight. Now stack the pieces up in order, tap the end of the deck to even up the cards and fasten them together at the notched end with a rubber band. Then just flip through the stack with your thumb to see the pictures move.

You can also make your own flipbooks. 3" x 5" index cards are good to use since they're stiffer than normal paper. Make up your own story and characters, then draw a series of action pictures on the cards.

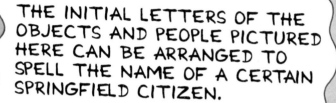

WHO IS IT?

OH, BROTHER!

THE INITIAL LETTERS OF THE OBJECTS AND PEOPLE PICTURED HERE CAN BE ARRANGED TO SPELL THE NAME OF A CERTAIN SPRINGFIELD CITIZEN.

ADMIRAL BART'S BATTLESHIP

A game for two. Each player draws two big squares on a piece of paper. Then draw nine lines across and down, like in the picture below. Write 1 through 10 along the top of each and A through J down the side. One big square is the Battle Area, the other is the Target Area. Without showing each other where, draw ten battleships on the Battle Area. Five ships cover two squares each and five cover one square each. Leave at least one square between ships.

Keep your papers hidden from each other throughout the game. Each player takes a turn being the attacker by calling out a number and a letter (like A6). If the other player has a whole ship on that square, he or she says "direct hit." The attacker marks a B on his or her Target Area. If part of a ship is on that square, the defender says "damaged." The attacker knows he or she has sunk only half a ship. If no ship is on the square, the attacker draws an X in the same square on his or her Target Area. Then the other player is the attacker. The winner is the first one to sink all the other player's battleships.

BATTLE AREA

TARGET AREA

DO YOU HAVE PRINCE ALBERT IN A CAN?*

WACKY TALKY TIN CANS

TAKE 2 EMPTY, CLEAN TIN CANS WITH ONE END CUT OUT. PUNCH A SMALL HOLE IN EACH BOTTOM. POKE ONE END OF A 20-FOOT LENGTH OF HEAVY COTTON STRING THROUGH EACH OF THE HOLES. TIE KNOTS IN THE ENDS TO KEEP THE STRING FROM PULLING THROUGH. YOU AND A FRIEND STAND FAR ENOUGH APART THAT THE STRING IS PULLED TIGHT. NOW TALK INTO ONE CAN WHILE YOUR FRIEND LISTENS AT THE OTHER END!

*ASK YOUR GRANDPA WHAT THIS MEANS.

Start with an 8 1/2" square piece of paper. Fold it in half diagonally both ways to find the center point (Fig. 1). Open up and fold each corner in to the center point (Fig. 2). Turn over and fold each corner of the smaller square in to the middle. Under each of these flaps, write an "answer": "Yeah, Man!," "No Way, Man! ," "Mmmaybe" and "Try Again." Or make up something. Write numbers on each of the flaps as shown (Fig. 3). Turn it over again and write numbers in each of the small triangular areas on that side (Fig. 4). Once again, turn it over. Now fold down the middle both ways to crease it. Push all four corners together and hold from the underside with the forefinger and thumb of each hand (Fig. 5). Your Mystical Fortune Teller is complete! Now have your friend ask a yes or no question and pick one of the numbers on the outside. Pull with the thumb and forefinger of one hand to open the center. Close it, then pull with the other two fingers to open the other way (Fig. 6). Go back and forth the number of times your friend picked. When you come to a stop ask him or her to pick one of the inside numbers and repeat the process. Finally, ask him or her to pick one more number. Open up the Fortune Teller and read the answer under that triangle.

YOUR FUTURE IS IN MY HANDS!

HUMAN SARDINES

One person hides, in a place with a little extra room - - an out-of-the-way closet or under a bed or table covered with a cloth. Everyone else searches for him or her. When someone finds the hiding place, he or she gets in too. One by one, the players disappear...until only one is left, the loser.

WHO SWIPED THE CUPCAKES

Marge had invited her sisters, Patty and Selma, over for a visit...just a little chit-chat and "girl talk." They said they'd be over around 2 o'clock.

The Simpsons had eaten a nutritious lunch a short while ago and there were two yummy cupcakes left over. "Mmmmm," said Marge. "I'll serve these to Patty and Selma when they arrive." She placed the cupcakes on a plate on the kitchen table and then went about cleaning up the kitchen. Maggie was crawling about on the floor, Lisa was quietly doing her homework, Bart was slurping on a "Big Burp" soda and Homer was milling about nearby.

Promptly at 2 o'clock the doorbell rang. "I'll get it," said Marge. "It must be my sisters!"

"Hooo-boy," moaned Homer. "Those two brighten a room just by leaving it!"

Marge put the dish she was washing in the dish rack and went to the front door. On her way past the kitchen table she checked once more on the two yummy cupcakes.

When Marge opened the door to greet Patty and Selma she realized she still had on her rubber dishwashing gloves. "Oh dear!" cried Marge. "Make yourselves at home, girls! I'll be right back!" When Marge dashed back into the kitchen she saw right away that the two cupcakes had disappeared. "Oh my word! In the mere 30 seconds I was out of this room someone swiped those two yummy cupcakes!"

The drawing shows the kitchen immediately upon Marge's return. Can you tell who swiped the cupcakes and how the thief tried to cover his or her tracks?

1. Was it easy for Maggie to grab the cupcakes?
2. Was it easy to Lisa to grab the cupcakes?
3. Was it easy for Bart to grab the cupcakes?
4. Was it easy for Homer to grab the cupcakes?
5. Do you see anyone else who might have taken them?
6. Do you see any place the cupcakes might be hidden?
7. Do you see any clue as to who might have hidden them there?
8. If so, who do you think swiped the cupcakes and how can you tell?

Solution on Page 62.

Lisa's HOUSE O' MYSTERIES

TREASURE HUNT

First, pick out a "treasure" and hide it somewhere in the house. Then, write the clues on pieces of paper and hide them around the house. Each clue tells where to find the next clue, right up to the treasure. The first clue is read aloud to all players. This hunt starts with: "I light up your life!"

MURDER
IN THE DARK

THIS IS A GOOD GAME FOR 5 OR MORE PLAYERS. FIRST, CUT SLIPS OF PAPER FOR EACH PLAYER. MARK AN "X" ON ONE PIECE AND A "D" ON ANOTHER. ALL THE REST ARE LEFT BLANK. FOLD THEM IN HALF AND HAVE EACH PLAYER TAKE ONE. THE PLAYER WITH THE "X" IS THE MURDERER. HE KEEPS IT A SECRET. "D" IS THE DETECTIVE. HE TELLS EVERYONE WHO HE IS.

NEXT, THE LIGHTS ARE TURNED OFF AND EVERYONE EXCEPT THE DETECTIVE HIDES. THE MURDERER SNEAKS UP ON A HIDDEN PLAYER AND WHISPERS "YOU'RE DEAD" AND RUNS OFF. THE VICTIM SCREAMS, THE LIGHTS ARE TURNED ON AND EVERYONE GATHERS AROUND HIM. THE DETECTIVE THEN ASKS QUESTIONS TO FIND OUT WHO DONE IT. ONLY THE MURDERER CAN LIE. THE DETECTIVE HAS 3 GUESSES TO IDENTIFY THE MURDERER.

DETECTIVE

TWO PLAYERS ARE SELECTED TO BE DETECTIVES. THEY ARE THEN SENT OUT OF THE ROOM. THE OTHERS CHOOSE AN OBJECT WHICH THE DETECTIVES WILL TRY TO DISCOVER. THIS CAN BE A BOOK, A CHAIR, PART OF SOMEONE'S CLOTHING OR ANYTHING IN THE ROOM. THE DETECTIVES ARE CALLED BACK IN AND TRY TO SOLVE THE MYSTERY BY ASKING QUESTIONS. THEY MAY ASK EACH PLAYER ONLY 3 QUESTIONS. HAVE THEM TRY TO FIND THE LOCATION FIRST, AND THEN ATTEMPT TO NAME THE OBJECT.

"I have SPOKE, but said nothing. Come AROUND and you'll find clue #3."

"I never move, yet you're always WATCHING ME. Look to me for clue #4."

ANSWER: The treasure is under "TREASURE" in the dictionary!

"I know all the WORDS, but I tell no story. Look me up and find the 'treasure'!"

"I have KEYS, but no locks. Take NOTE and you'll discover your next clue."

PENCIL PAGE

HANGMAN

One player is the executioner. The other is the convict. The executioner thinks of a 6- or 7-letter word and marks down a dash for each letter on some paper. The convict tries to guess, one by one, the letters that make up the word. For each wrong guess, the executioner draws in a part of the gallows or the hanging man. First the gallows, then the rope, then the head, the face, the body, the left arm, the right arm, the left leg and the right leg. If the convict guesses a letter in the word, the executioner writes it in position on the dash. If the convict guesses the whole word before he is hanged, he wins. If not, the executioner wins. If you choose an especially long or tough word, you can add more body parts (ears, eyes, etc.) to give the convict a reprieve on his sentence.

1	2		3	4	5	6		7	8	9	10
11	12	13		14	15	16		17	18	19	
20	21	22	23		24	25	26		27	28	29

DOUBLE ACROSTIC: ANSWER EACH OF THE QUESTIONS BELOW. THEN ENTER THE LETTERS INTO THE BOXES ABOVE ACCORDING TO THE NUMBERS INDICATED.

A. Word before dog or foot or rod.
 ‾15‾ ‾12‾ ‾6‾

B. Weak; spineless.
 ‾14‾ ‾1‾ ‾9‾ ‾10‾ ‾27‾

C. Head of the House of Simpson.
 ‾20‾ ‾16‾ ‾2‾ ‾26‾ ‾5‾

D. What Bart is to the above.
 ‾7‾ ‾28‾ ‾13‾

E. John or Paul or George or Ringo.
 ‾3‾ ‾19‾ ‾24‾ ‾17‾ ‾23‾ ‾21‾

F. Ben's last name.
 ‾18‾ ‾29‾ ‾25‾

G. Simpson sibling.
 ‾22‾ ‾8‾ ‾11‾ ‾4‾

Solutions on page 62 .

WHOEVER REACHES THE TV FIRST GETS TO PICK THE CHANNEL. WILL IT BE AMERICA'S MOST ARMED AND DANGEROUS OR *THE HAPPY LITTLE ELVES?*

The Simpsons Take a Road Trip

Write each item from the list on a 3" x 5" index card and deal the cards out to all the players. The narrator reads the story, pausing at the blanks. In turn, each player reads a card to fill in the missing words.

The List

- a cheap cigar
- a space mutant
- six fur balls
- a snide remark
- a knuckle sandwich
- a smug poodle
- a tofu salad
- a ridiculous hair style
- a frozen pizza
- a screaming lunatic
- a jar of dirt
- a cow pie
- two stupid cats
- a garden slug
- a wharf rat
- a young Republican
- a pain in the butt
- a nuclear bomb
- an excitable hamster
- a rusted accordion
- a big, phony smile
- a greasy doorknob
- forty-two jelly donuts
- a dull thud
- a smelly, old sock

The Story

Like it or not, it's time for the Simpsons' annual vacation road trip. Or, as Bart calls it, "Bummer in the Summer." Homer has loaded up the car with _____, _____ and _____. And Marge has prepared _____, _____ and _____ to eat along the way.

Soon they're all packed up and heading down the highway. "Oh, look!" says Lisa, pointing out the window. "There's a car with _____ strapped to its roof!" "They must be from California," reasons Marge.

"Dad, I'm so hungry I could eat_____!" says Bart. "Let's stop at that Weenie Barn up ahead!" Homer pulls in and everyone piles out of the car. "I'll get us a booth near _____," says Bart as he charges into the restaurant.

"Welcome to Weenie Barn," says the waitress. "Today's special is _____ served on _____. So, what kin I get youse guys?" "I'll have _____, _____ and _____!" shouts Bart. "And I'll have _____, _____ and_____," says Lisa. "Cool it, you two." says Homer. "Your eyes are bigger than your stomachs. We'll just have _____ each and a side of juicy fries," says Marge. "Oh, and _____ for Maggie."

The scrumptious meal is quickly eaten. "C'mon," says Homer. "I wanna put in another 200 miles before dark." Unfortunately, when they all get back in the car, it won't start. "Sounds like you got _____in the carburetor, Dad," observes Bart. "Drat!" curses Homer. "I KNEW I shoulda put _____in the radiator before we left!" "Yes, dear," says Marge calmly. "That's why I put a spare one in the trunk."

PICNIC PANIC!

Those darn bears have scattered 24 items from the
Simpsons' picnic all over the woods! Can you help find them all?

CUT ALONG LINES. ATTACH A TO A AND B TO B.

INSTRUCTIONS

2. TAPE

FOLD

1. PASTE THE CIRCLE ONTO CARDBOARD AND CUT OUT.

2. CUT OUT THE TWO STRIPS ON THE NEXT PAGE, BEING SURE TO CUT OUT EACH OF THE LITTLE SLITS, TOO. TAPE THE STRIPS TOGETHER AND FOLD UP THE BOTTOM TABS AS SHOWN.

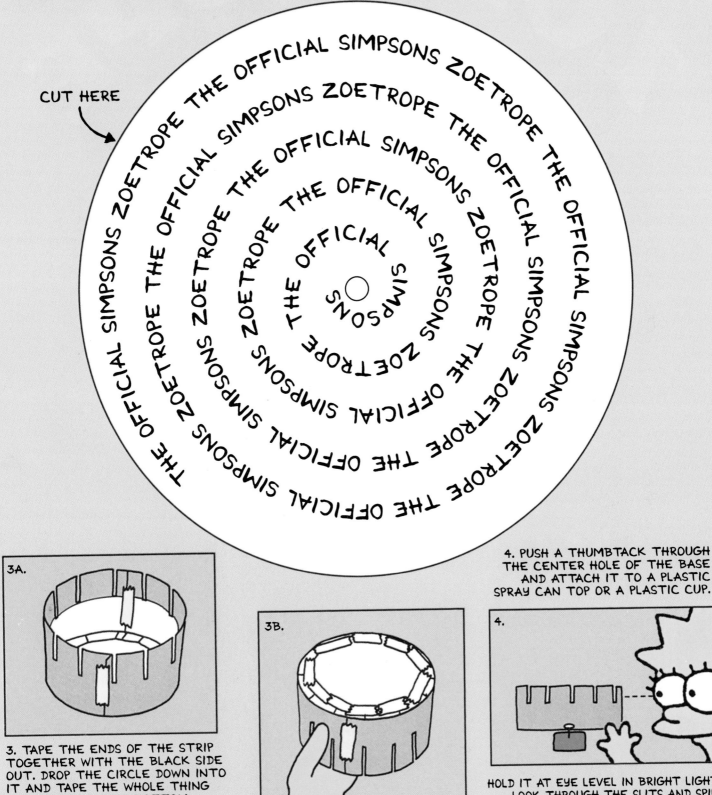

CUT HERE

THE OFFICIAL SIMPSONS ZOETROPE

3A.

3. TAPE THE ENDS OF THE STRIP TOGETHER WITH THE BLACK SIDE OUT. DROP THE CIRCLE DOWN INTO IT AND TAPE THE WHOLE THING TOGETHER ON THE BOTTOM.

3B.

4. PUSH A THUMBTACK THROUGH THE CENTER HOLE OF THE BASE AND ATTACH IT TO A PLASTIC SPRAY CAN TOP OR A PLASTIC CUP.

4.

HOLD IT AT EYE LEVEL IN BRIGHT LIGHT, LOOK THROUGH THE SLITS AND SPIN!

5. FOR MORE MOVING PICTURES, CUT OUT THE OTHER STRIPS ON THE FOLLOWING PAGES AND TAPE THEM TOGETHER AS INDICATED. PLACE ONE OF THEM INSIDE THE "WHEEL OF LIFE" AND SPIN AS YOU DID BEFORE. TO SEE THE OTHER SIDES OF THE STRIPS, CUT THE TAPE, TURN THE STRIP AROUND AND TAPE IT AGAIN.

Pointless Trivia

MAGGIE'S MIXED-UP PICTURE SCRAMBLE

MAGGIE'S BEST, BEST PAL IN THE WHOLE WIDE WORLD IS A FABULOUS MONSTER!
IT HAS FOUR LEGS, TWO EARS AND ONE GREAT BIG EYE THAT STARES AND GLARES BUT NEVER SEES. CUT
THESE PIECES APART AND UNSCRAMBLE THE PICTURE PUZZLE TO DISCOVER MAGGIE'S BEASTLY FRIEND.

Solution on Page 62.

Self-Inflating MIRACLE BALLOON

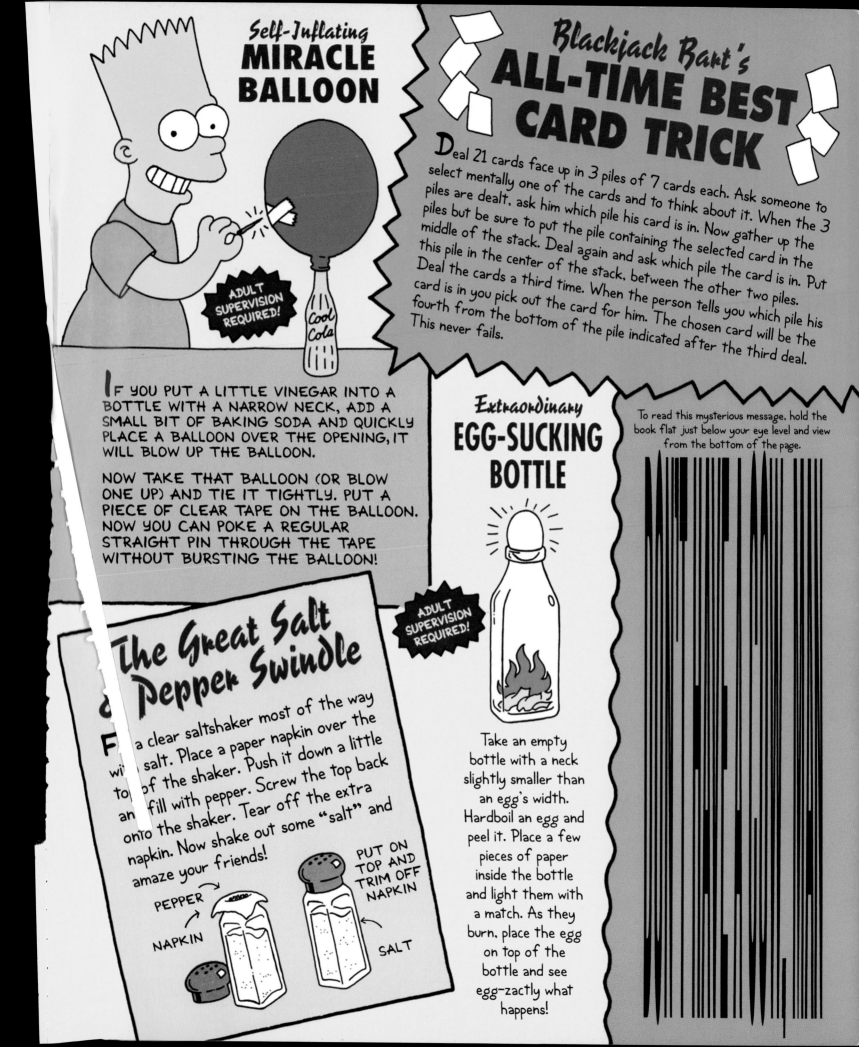

ADULT SUPERVISION REQUIRED!

IF YOU PUT A LITTLE VINEGAR INTO A BOTTLE WITH A NARROW NECK, ADD A SMALL BIT OF BAKING SODA AND QUICKLY PLACE A BALLOON OVER THE OPENING, IT WILL BLOW UP THE BALLOON.

NOW TAKE THAT BALLOON (OR BLOW ONE UP) AND TIE IT TIGHTLY. PUT A PIECE OF CLEAR TAPE ON THE BALLOON. NOW YOU CAN POKE A REGULAR STRAIGHT PIN THROUGH THE TAPE WITHOUT BURSTING THE BALLOON!

Blackjack Bart's ALL-TIME BEST CARD TRICK

Deal 21 cards face up in 3 piles of 7 cards each. Ask someone to select mentally one of the cards and to think about it. When the 3 piles are dealt, ask him which pile his card is in. Now gather up the piles but be sure to put the pile containing the selected card in the middle of the stack. Deal again and ask which pile the card is in. Put this pile in the center of the stack, between the other two piles. Deal the cards a third time. When the person tells you which pile his card is in you pick out the card for him. The chosen card will be the fourth from the bottom of the pile indicated after the third deal. This never fails.

Extraordinary EGG-SUCKING BOTTLE

ADULT SUPERVISION REQUIRED!

To read this mysterious message, hold the book flat just below your eye level and view from the bottom of the page.

Take an empty bottle with a neck slightly smaller than an egg's width. Hardboil an egg and peel it. Place a few pieces of paper inside the bottle and light them with a match. As they burn, place the egg on top of the bottle and see egg-zactly what happens!

The Great Salt Pepper Swindle

...a clear saltshaker most of the way with salt. Place a paper napkin over the top of the shaker. Push it down a little and fill with pepper. Screw the top back onto the shaker. Tear off the extra napkin. Now shake out some "salt" and amaze your friends!

PEPPER →

NAPKIN

PUT ON TOP AND TRIM OFF NAPKIN

SALT

OH NO! YOU'VE BROKEN EVERY BONE IN YOUR NOSE!

PLACE YOUR PALMS TOGETHER, FINGERS POINTING UP, AND GRIP YOUR NOSE BETWEEN YOUR TWO FOREFINGERS. PUT THE THUMBNAIL OF YOUR RIGHT HAND BEHIND YOUR UPPER FRONT TEETH. TWIST YOUR NOSE TO ONE SIDE WITH YOUR FOREFINGERS AND, AT THE SAME TIME, CLICK YOUR THUMBNAIL ON YOUR TEETH BY PRESSING YOUR THUMB FORWARD.

Mesmerizing X-RAY HAND

Roll a piece of paper into a thin tube and hold it up to one eye while keeping both eyes open. Hold it with one hand and place your other hand with the palm facing you, so that the side of the hand is touching the tube. Remember to keep both eyes open. As you look through the tube, move your hand toward you and away from you until you can see a hole in the middle of your hand.

Mystical MELDING GLASSES

USE TWO GLASSES THAT ARE THE SAME SIZE. PUT A CANDLE IN THE BOTTOM GLASS. LIGHT IT AND PLACE A THICK PIECE OF WET PAPER OVER IT. NOW PUT THE OTHER GLASS ON TOP AS SHOWN. THE CANDLE WILL GO OUT AND THE GLASSES WILL BE STUCK TOGETHER. TO TAKE APART, RUN UNDER HOT WATER.

ADULT SUPERVISION REQUIRED!

Confusing FUSING STRINGS

USE ONE LONG AND ONE SHORT STRING. FOLD THEM BOTH IN HALF AND HOLD THEM IN YOUR HAND AS IN ILLUSTRATION #1. CLOSE YOUR HAND TO SHOW. IT WILL LOOK LIKE PICTURE #2. PUT THE STRINGS IN YOUR POCKET WITH THE LONG ENDS HANGING OUT. PULL THE STRING BY ONE END. THE SHORT PIECE STAYS IN YOUR POCKET.

1.
2.
3.
4.

BAFFLE YOUR FRIENDS WITH THE AMAZING Reappearing NUMBER

THINK OF A NUMBER BETWEEN 1 AND 100, MULTIPLY BY 2, ADD 10, DIVIDE BY 2, AND SUBTRACT THE NUMBER YOU THOUGHT OF. THE ANSWER IS 5 NO MATTER WHAT NUMBER YOU CHOOSE.

5 9 7 ÷ + 12 3 8 = 2 6 ×

KRUSTY'S
3 RINGS-O-FUN!

BALLOON VOLLEYBALL

Stretch a string across the room to be the net. Divide players into two groups -- one on either side of the string. Throw an inflated balloon in play. Each group bats the ball in the air, trying to keep the balloon from touching the floor on their side. They bat it back and forth over the string with their hands. Each time the balloon hits the floor, the opposing team scores one point. The game is 10 points.

SHOES AND SOCK-ER

Take about six shoes of all different sizes and line them up in three rows. Now, get three small pairs of socks -- not too smelly, or you'll be fouled outta the game! Roll each pair tightly into a ball and put a rubber band around each sock-ball. One at a time, toss the socks into the shoes. The smallest shoes are the hardest to hit, so those score the highest points. High score wins.

TIN CAN BOWL-A-RAMA

Set up 10 "bowling pins" using plastic bottles or tin cans in a triangle. Players take turns rolling a small ball to knock the pins down. Score one point for each pin. If all the pins are knocked down with one throw, add 10 to the number of pins the same player knocks down on his or her next turn. Each player gets 10 rolls. The high score wins.

SOLUTION ON PAGE 62.

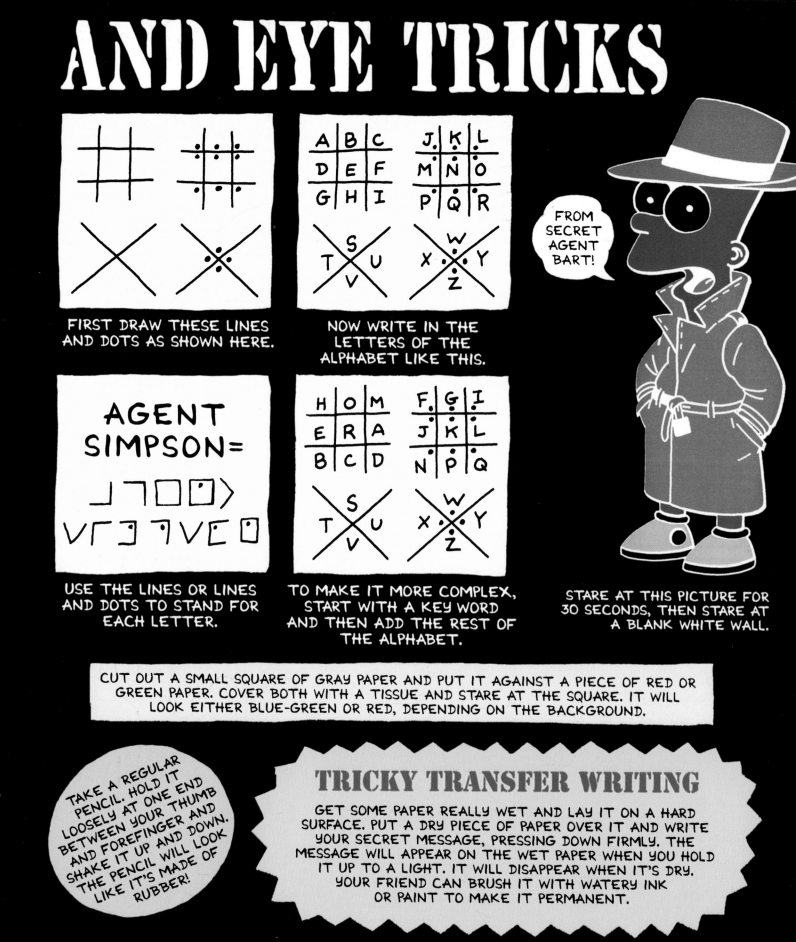

FIRST DRAW THESE LINES AND DOTS AS SHOWN HERE.

NOW WRITE IN THE LETTERS OF THE ALPHABET LIKE THIS.

AGENT SIMPSON=

USE THE LINES OR LINES AND DOTS TO STAND FOR EACH LETTER.

TO MAKE IT MORE COMPLEX, START WITH A KEY WORD AND THEN ADD THE REST OF THE ALPHABET.

FROM SECRET AGENT BART!

STARE AT THIS PICTURE FOR 30 SECONDS, THEN STARE AT A BLANK WHITE WALL.

CUT OUT A SMALL SQUARE OF GRAY PAPER AND PUT IT AGAINST A PIECE OF RED OR GREEN PAPER. COVER BOTH WITH A TISSUE AND STARE AT THE SQUARE. IT WILL LOOK EITHER BLUE-GREEN OR RED, DEPENDING ON THE BACKGROUND.

TAKE A REGULAR PENCIL. HOLD IT LOOSELY AT ONE END BETWEEN YOUR THUMB AND FOREFINGER AND SHAKE IT UP AND DOWN. THE PENCIL WILL LOOK LIKE IT'S MADE OF RUBBER!

TRICKY TRANSFER WRITING

GET SOME PAPER REALLY WET AND LAY IT ON A HARD SURFACE. PUT A DRY PIECE OF PAPER OVER IT AND WRITE YOUR SECRET MESSAGE, PRESSING DOWN FIRMLY. THE MESSAGE WILL APPEAR ON THE WET PAPER WHEN YOU HOLD IT UP TO A LIGHT. IT WILL DISAPPEAR WHEN IT'S DRY. YOUR FRIEND CAN BRUSH IT WITH WATERY INK OR PAINT TO MAKE IT PERMANENT.

SECRET SPY TRICKS

GIVE THESE OPTICAL ILLUSIONS A TRY. YOU MIGHT BE SURPRISED BY THE ANSWERS!

A
B
C
D

1. Which lines are parallel?
A___ B___ C___ D___

A   B   C

2. Which of these lines is the longest?
A___ B___ C___

3. Is this hat higher than it is wide?
Yes___ No___

A   B   C   D   E   F   G   H   I

4. Which is the longest line?
A___ B___ C___ D___ E___
F___ G___ H___ I___

A   B

5. Which inner circle is the larger?   A____ B____

Answers on Page 64.

HANDY HAND ALPHABET

END OF WORD.

USE THE HAND SIGNALS BELOW TO SEND SECRET MESSAGES TO A FRIEND WHO ALSO KNOWS THEM. WHEN YOU'RE AT THE END OF A WORD, MOVE YOUR HAND BACK AND FORTH WITH YOUR PALM FACE DOWN. DO THE SAME THING WITH BOTH HANDS TO SIGNAL THE END OF A SENTENCE. TRY USING SHORTHAND FOR SOME LETTERS LIKE A "C" FOR THE WORD "SEE" OR A "U" FOR THE WORD "YOU."

END OF SENTENCE.

INVISIBLE INK

You can use milk, lemon juice or vinegar for ink. Or you can make a solution of 1/2 cup water and 1/2 cup sugar or salt. Use a matchstick, brush or cotton swab as a pen. Write on regular paper and let it dry. Your correspondent can read the message by pressing the paper with a slightly warm iron or putting it near a lighted electric bulb.

A	B	C	D	E	F	G	H	I	J	K	L	M

IT TAKES 113 POUNDS OF $20 BILLS TO MAKE $1 MILLION DOLLARS.

MR. BURNS

A BIRD'S FEATHERS CAN WEIGH UP TO TWICE AS MUCH AS ITS SKELETON.

THE VIKINGS COLONIZED ALL OF SICILY.

IN SPRINGFIELD THERE ONCE WAS A CLOWN WHOSE FACE NEVER WORE A GRIM FROWN. "FOR LIFE I AM NUTSY," CRIED LOVABLE KRUSTY, "SO WHY NOT SPREAD MY JOY AROUND?"

ELEPHANTS KILL MORE PEOPLE EVERY YEAR THAN DO SHARKS.

SMITHERS

THE BLOOD PRESSURE OF HUMANS IS ABOUT THE SAME AS THAT OF SPIDERS.

KRUSTY

BLEEDING GUMS MURPHY

SOME HENS LAY EGGS SHAPED LIKE CUCUMBERS.

MONKEYS LOVE ONIONS.

SHERRI & TERRI

IN TOLEDO, OHIO, IT IS ILLEGAL TO THROW A SNAKE.

SOUTH AMERICA WAS CALLED AMERICA BEFORE NORTH AMERICA.

SIDESHOW BOB

PORCUPINES COMMUNICATE WITH EACH OTHER BY CLICKING THEIR TEETH.

TV SET

85 PERCENT OF GUNSHOTS FIRED IN TV SHOWS MISS.

Who says you have to be a bigshot Hollywood producer to have your own TV show? Now you can do it yourself at home! It's much cheaper and easier than the real thing, and there are no pesky actors, writers, or unions to deal with! Just cut out these figures along the dotted lines (you can make 'em sturdier by gluing the pages onto thin cardboard before you cut them out); then cut a little slit in the base and the crosspiece where the lines are. Slide the crosspiece into the base, and presto—your cast is ready for action. Next, find a cardboard box about the size of this book. Cut a hole that's a little smaller than a page in one side of the box. Cut out the screen from the TV on the back of this page (finish reading these instructions first!) and tape the TV on the cut-out side of the box, like in the picture here. Tape a background (school, living room, or draw your own) to the inside of the back of the box, and your TV show is ready to air. The only thing missing is the remote control!

and social success!" claims my brother. You have been warned. Grampa's ZOETROPE—This thing is so old it's new! PICNIC PANIC—Yep. It's one of them pesky hidden picture puzzles. ESCAPE FROM 4TH GRADE—Join Bart for a casual stroll home from school. ROAD TRIP—Say WHAT?! Call the auto club, man . . . we're having a communication breakdown! PENCIL PAGE—Better put on your thinking caps for this one. Some clean socks wouldn't hurt, either. LISA'S HOUSE O' MYSTERIES—Prepare to be baffled, if not irked and peeved. WHO SWIPED THE CUPCAKES?—A chilling, real-life tale of greed and larceny . . . starring all your favorite Simpsons. MADAME LISA'S MYSTICAL FORTUNE TELLER, WACKY TALKY TIN CANS, HUMAN SARDINES, ADMIRAL BART'S BATTLESHIP and WHO IS IT?—A cornucopia of miscellaneous grab-bag surprises and tomfoolery. Too complicated to explain. SIDESHOW BOB'S FLIPPED OUT FLIPBOOK—An inside look at how a convicted felon passes his time behind bars. SPITBALL DART BOARD—The Sport of Kings. MARGE'S WEEK-AT-A-GLANCE—And you thought she was just a housewife! OTTO'S WILD RIDE—Fasten your seat belts, dudes. We're outta here! HANDY SHADOW SHOWS, SILHOUETTES and SPINNING SPIRAL THINGY. PAPER-MANIA—A collection of basic paper tricks on which to build an entire repertoire of parlor games and stunts. Some real crowd-pleasers. MESSIN' UP THE KITCHEN—It was at this point in the book that we all got hungry and went into the kitchen for a bite to eat! THE OFFICIAL HECK-OF-A-DECK SIMPSONS PLAYING CARDS—Some of the all-time great card games of the Western world . . . and a deck of Simpsons' cards to play 'em with. SOLUTIONS TO PUZZLES—Why not do what Homer does? Start reading the book here!

HELP! GET ME HOME, MAN!

FOOD? DID I HEAR SOMEONE MENTION FOOD?

Does all this sound too good to be true? You bet it is!

We hope this book will provide you with hours & hours of the same Simpson-style mental activity that went into creating it.

Have a Rainy Day!

Lisa Simpson

Lisa Simpson of
The Simpsons

THE SIMPSONS
RAINY DAY FUN BOOK

Introduction by Lisa Simpson

We Simpsons have long been devotees of mindless entertainment. So when the good folks at HarperCollins suggested we put together a Rainy Day Fun Book, our first reaction was "How useful! How productive! How boring!"

We'd seen these so-called fun books before -- scientific projects, mind-altering picture puzzles, educational card games. "Fun" indeed! Not for us these worthwhile pastimes. No way.

What then, thought we, might be done to put the "F" back in fun? Why not create a new-age rainy day book with nothing whatsoever useful in it? Why not a book that's nearly as devoid of purpose as an evening of television? A book crammed with fun and fun by-products, with no redeeming educational value or significant political undercurrents. A SIMPSONS Rainy Day Fun Book.

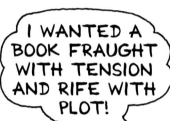

I WANTED A BOOK FRAUGHT WITH TENSION AND RIFE WITH PLOT!

And here's what we've stuffed it full of:
PUT ON YOUR OWN TV SHOW—Be your own Network Programmer! Write your own scripts! Cancel your own series! GOOFY GOLF—We haven't seen links this goofy since there was that explosion at the sausage factory! (Bart wrote that last joke.) SECRET SPY TRICKS AND EYE TRICKS—Lotsa top-secret stuff left over from the Cold War.

WELL, I FEEL IT SHOULD HAVE SOME EDUCATIONAL VALUE.

Just reheat and serve. GO NUTS FOR DONUTS—Out there it's dog-eat-dog, but here at the Simpsons', just the reverse is true! KRUSTY'S 3 RINGS-O-FUN—We promise, not one dime from this book will go into that clown's pocket! BART & LISA'S MAGIC SHOW—The title tells all. HOMER-DINI AGE-GUESSER—Ta da! No age too awkward! Amazing, and not the least bit enlightening! MAGGIE'S MIXED-UP PICTURE SCRAMBLE—No, it's not much of a puzzle, but she's just a child, for goshsakes! POINTLESS TRIVIA—"Commit these to memory and you will enjoy lifelong popularity

TO THE MEMORY
OF SNOWBALL I

YOU MAY BE GONE,
BUT YOUR MIDNIGHT YOWLING
STILL ECHOES IN OUR EARS.

THE SIMPSONS RAINY DAY FUN BOOK was originally published in 1991 by HarperPerennial, a Division of HarperCollins Publishers. Copyright© 1991 by Matt Groening Productions, inc.

THE SIMPSONS FUN IN THE SUN BOOK was originally published in 1992 by HarperPerennial, a Division of HarperCollins Publishers. Copyright© 1992 by Matt Groening Productions, inc.

THE SIMPSONS ULTRA-JUMBO RAIN-OR-SHINE FUN BOOK. Copyright © 1993 by Matt Groening Productions, inc. All rights reserved. Printed in the United States of America. No part of this book may be used or reproduced in any manner whatsoever without written permission except in the case of brief quotations embodied in critical articles and reviews. For information address HarperCollins Publishers, 10 East 53rd Street, New York, NY 10022.

HarperCollins books may be purchased for educational, business, or sales promotional use. For information please write: Special Markets Department, HarperCollins Publishers, 10 East 53rd Street, New York, NY 10022.

First Harper paperback published 2006.

ISBN-10: 0-06-095006-4
ISBN-13: 978-0-06-095006-4

06 07 08 09 10 RRD 10 9 8 7 6 5 4 3 2

Concepts, Design & Art Direction: Cindy Vance
Rainy Day Fun Team: Mary Trainor (Captain), Steve Vance, and Dyan Sheldon
Design Associate: Peter Alexander
Production Assistant: Clare O'Callaghan
Illustration: Bill Morrison, John Adams, and Steve Vance
Color Separations & Printing: R.R. Donnelley & Sons

MATT GROENING'S

THE SIMPSONS

RAINY DAY

FUN
BOOK

HARPER

NEW YORK • LONDON • TORONTO • SYDNEY